Close To Home

Cara Johnson

Whirling Dirvish Publishing

Published by

Whirling Dirvish Publishing

26895 Aliso Creek Road #B591
Aliso Viejo, CA 92656

Design and layout
RJ Communications
51 East 42nd Street, Suite 1202
New York, New York 10017

Cover illustration by Hye Seong Yoon

Library of Congress Control Number: 2009922527

ISBN 13: 978-0-9768870-5-8 (paperback)

Printed in the United States of America

For Charlie and Pahoma

Contents

One	Discovered	7
Two	Questions	12
Three	Brothers	24
Four	Wide Awake	39
Five	On the Road	50
Six	Now and Then	65
Seven	In the Fields	79
Eight	Lost	95
Nine	Pahoma	110
Ten	Nightmare	126
Eleven	Change	142
Twelve	Into the Light	161

Chapter 1

Discovered

Anna lay in her bed listening. It was late—that she knew for sure. Outside her window the blackened night sky cast an eerie shadow over everything. And of course, there was the stillness that only the middle of the night brought—the time when all were fast asleep. Well, almost all. Anna turned her head on her pillow and listened some more.

Something was not quite right in her room. She couldn't really put her finger on what it was, but it had been bothering her for days. It had all started last week when she'd walked into her room and it felt as if something or someone was watching her. Anna turned around, expecting to find her mother in the room with her. "Mom?" she called out. But she realized, almost instantly, that she was alone.

The first time it happened, Anna had brushed it off with a shake of her head and an easy chuckle. But when it continued to happen, her easy chuckles turned to nervous laughs and then hasty exits from her bedroom.

It wasn't until some of her prized possessions began disappearing that Anna started listening. First it was her pink fuzzy feather pen. Then it was her purple and pink striped locking diary notebook (which she never locked because the lock had broken months ago). And, finally, her Falling Awake book (the one Mama Do-Right had given her to help her learn how to Dream Travel). When the book vanished, Anna knew *something* was up. She'd searched high and low and found none of her treasured things, and the weird feeling of not being alone in her room persisted.

But why was she listening? And listening for what? Anna struggled to answer her own questions as she lay on her back in bed staring at the ceiling above her. Maybe, she hedged, because she'd had no luck when *looking*, she'd have more luck when *listening*. She shrugged at her own response. *Or maybe*, she added, *I've completely lost my mind along with my pink fuzzy feather pen, my purple and pink locking diary notebook, and my Falling Awake book.* Anna drew a long breath.

That's when she heard it. It was slight—a quiet rustling—but it caught Anna's attention. She pulled her head up from the pillow.

The room was deadly silent for a long moment and then Anna heard it once more. The rustling sound was louder this time. It almost sounded as if someone was turning pages in a book. But more strange than the sound she heard was where the sound was coming from. Anna stared her closet door with wide frightened eyes. Something. . . or someone. . . was behind that door.

Anna's body turned as stiff as wood. She tried to fight back her fear with rational thoughts. *It's probably a toy rolling around in there,* she thought. Or maybe the air conditioning was making things sway in her closet. *Or, or...* Anna exhaled. Her explanations were pitiful and she knew it. She had no toys that rolled and she was almost positive the air conditioning was not on. Her was room toasty warm.

Again the rustling noise echoed from behind her closet door. It was even louder than before.

Anna pinched her eyes shut. She stayed like that for what felt like forever and then slowly she opened her eyes. *I have to get out of bed,* she thought. *I have to get out of bed, open the closet door, and see what's making that noise.* Anna silently groaned at her own plan. The last thing she wanted to do was to get out of bed and go anywhere near that closet door. But she really didn't see that she had a choice.

Anna bit her lip. Dread rolled through her rigid body in waves. Another moment passed and then, robotically, she pushed her covers down and swung her legs off the edge of her bed. She gulped once and then, quiet as a cat, she hopped onto her bedroom floor. Anna allowed herself one small exhale before starting the long tip-toe to her closet.

When she heard the noise again from behind her closet door, Anna stopped in her tracks and winced. And then a truly wonderful thought came to her. *Wait a minute,* she mused, *maybe it's a mouse or something.* Normally the idea of a small rodent rifling through her things would not give her joy, but she was so relieved to have found a logical explanation that her body released its tight grip, and her face split into a wide smile. *Of course,* she added, *that even explains why I have felt like something or someone was watching me!* "It's a mouse," she whispered. *It's gotta be,* her mind echoed.

Anna spun on her heels searching in the darkness of her room for something long enough and large enough to wound—or at *least* scare—the pesky mouse. She spotted the perfect tool almost immediately. Propped up next to her dresser was her softball bat. *Yeah,* she thought, *Perfect!* Anna quickly retrieved the bat and, with renewed confidence, padded quietly over to her closet door.

Anna reached the door in matter of seconds, lifted the bat in the air with her right hand, and with her left hand she grabbed the closet door handle. "Get ready for a big headache, mouse!" Anna whispered. She opened the door dramatically, her eyes narrowed, prepared for battle. But what she found on the other side of that door shocked her more than a thousand mice could have.

Sitting Indian style, on the floor of her closet, with her pink fuzzy feather pen behind one of his ears, her purple and pink striped locking diary notebook propped in his lap, and her Falling Awake book creased open in his hands was a boy—a small, blond-haired boy, probably no more than eight years old. He took one look at Anna and smiled.

"I want to fall awake," he said innocently. And then immediately, he disappeared.

Anna made to scream, but in a heartbeat she found herself jerking up from her pillow. She was back in her bed. She covered her mouth in horror. *What was that? Was I dreaming? Was I awake? Am I awake now?*

But more important than all of those questions combined, was the one question that had Anna twisting her head towards the center of her room.

"Who is in my closet!"

Chapter 2

Questions

Anna sat on her bedroom floor with her knees drawn up towards her chest and watched—rolling her eyes in waves of annoyance—as Alex paced the floor in front of her. She was well past the point of regretting her decision to tell him about the boy in her closet. In fact, if she had the energy to stand, she would be kicking herself this very moment. It was hovering close to noon and they had been at this since breakfast.

Alex stopped his pacing, hurriedly opened the small notebook he held in his left hand, and grabbed at the pencil stashed behind his ear. Anna—in the middle of another eye roll—stopped and waited. Maybe Alex had finally figured out how a complete stranger mysteriously wound up in her closet and then—just as mysteriously—disappeared. But a moment later, Alex shook his head, closed the notebook, and shoved the pencil back behind his ear.

When he began pacing again, Anna stifled a moan. "Alex," Anna started. He cut her off with a brisk wave of his hand. Anna's eyes narrowed. "Alex," she said again—this time more forcefully. Alex grabbed his pencil again and quickly scribbled something down in his notebook. Then he walked over to Anna's closet and opened the door. Anna dropped her head to her knees.

"So you found the boy here?" Alex pointed inside the closet. Anna slowly shook her head back and forth.

Alex gave her a confused look. "Wait, but you said you found him inside the closet." Flustered, Alex began flipping back through the notes he'd written in his notebook.

Anna let out an exasperated sigh and then looked up from her knees. "Alex, are you kidding me? You've asked me that same question like twenty times. The answer is YES!" she screamed. "For the last time, I found the boy *in* my closet!"

Now it was Alex who was rolling his eyes. "Anna, if you didn't want my help, then why did you call me?" He looked at Anna and raised his eyebrows in question.

Anna let out another exasperated sigh. "Honestly, I really didn't have anyone else to call. And besides, you're smart. Or at least I thought you were before you started asking me the same stupid questions over and over again. I mean, what does it matter *where* I found the boy? There was a *boy* in my closet... in the middle of the night! And then he like—just disappeared!"

Ignoring Anna's outburst, Alex walked into the closet, bent down, and picked up the fuzzy pink feather pen, the purple and pink stripped diary, and the Falling Awake book. "Obviously, it's an assignment, Anna," he said, matter-of-factly.

"Great," Anna said dryly, "now we get to go through that argument again." She uncurled her legs and stretched her back. "As I said—like a zillion times—assignments don't come to me. I go to them. That's how it works. Besides, you should know that. You've been on enough assignments with me by now to know that's how it happens."

Alex shrugged. "When it comes to Mama Do-Right and assignments, nothing is ever for sure. And that's the only thing I know for sure." Alex held up the pen, the diary, and the book and inspected them as if they were moon rocks. "So when the boy disappeared, these things just like—what? Fell down out of the air? Floated down?" Alex continued to study them as he waited for Anna's answer.

But Anna didn't answer. She didn't even let out an exaggerated huff or roll her eyes, which normally she would have, since Alex had already asked her that same question three other times. No, Anna didn't answer. And not because she was ignoring Alex or feeling frustrated. Anna didn't answer Alex's question because she was forming one of her own. What if Alex was right? What if the boy had been sent to her by…

Mama Do-Right, she thought. The strange and curious old woman who had turned Anna and Alex's lives upside down. It had been a little more than a year since Mama Do-Right had showed up in their world. In fact, she had appeared just months after Anna's father had died. Claiming to be a teacher, guide, and messenger from The New World, Mama Do-Right quickly proved herself to be all three and more. And within days of her arrival, Anna (and Alex) had agreed to work with The Council (the eyes and ears of The New World) helping other children who were in need. Even more fantastic than what they had agreed to was how they were to help the children.

"You're a Dream Traveler," Mama Do-Right had told Anna. "You have a natural gift." And as for Alex—Anna's best friend since birth and the smartest person she knew (probably the smartest person most people knew since he was considered a child genius)—he was tasked with helping Anna. In fact, he got so good at helping Anna with her assignments that he began Dream Traveling with her. The memory of Miko and Maka washed over Anna. *But that is just it,* thought Anna, shaking free of her memories. *We travel* to *our assignments.* It had always been the same. Why would it change now? It couldn't. It just wouldn't make any sense.

"Impossible," Anna whispered.

"What's impossible?" Alex was out of the closet again. He had left the pen, the diary, and the book where he had found them. No sense disturbing evidence, he thought. So far, they were the only clues he and Anna had. Alex was about to repeat his question when he glanced at Anna. In a heartbeat, he completely lost his train of thought.

"Anna," he asked worriedly, "what is it?"

Anna scratched her forehead and tried to hide the unease she suddenly felt. "Nothing... I... it's nothing..."

"Nothing?" Alex gave her a look. "You must really think I'm a moron if you expect me to believe 'nothing'. C'mon, spit it out."

"It doesn't make any sense." Anna was talking more to herself than to Alex. "Mama Do-Right doesn't send assignments to me. She just doesn't." Anna looked over at Alex. "She just doesn't!" she repeated, her voice cracking with emotion.

"Until now," Alex said calmly.

Anna moaned and instead of rolling her eyes, she rolled her entire head. "What makes you so sure it's an assignment?" she demanded.

Alex took in a long breath and then sat down quietly in front of Anna. "It's the only explanation that makes any sense."

Anna reached out and squeezed Alex's knee. "But you see," she said, "it doesn't make sense. It just doesn't."

Alex patted Anna's hand. "It does, Anna. When you add up all the facts, it's the only explanation that works."

"But you're wrong, Alex. I wasn't dreaming,

remember?"

Alex cleared his throat, grabbed for his pencil, and opened his notebook. "Bear with me," he said. "I just want to walk through the events of last night as you told them to me."

"Alex, we've been through this a hundred times—"

Alex put up his hand. "I know. I know we've been through it, but just bear with me this one last time."

"Do I have a choice?" Anna asked dryly.

Alex shrugged. "No, not really."

"Yah, great," she said, rolling her eyes.

Alex gave her a small smile. "I am glad you are so agreeable."

"Ha-Ha," she mocked. "Let's just get on with it."

Alex cleared his throat and began. "Okay, so for roughly a week you have felt like someone or something was in your room. And it wasn't your mother and you don't have pets—so we can rule those out."

"Alex," Anna interrupted, "are you for real? We *know* who was in the room. We've—"

Alex cut her off. "Anna, you promised to play nice and give me this one last time to go through all the facts. So retract your claws and relax. This is important." He shot her a parental stare and Anna scowled.

"I didn't promise to be nice," she mumbled under her breath.

Alex—who hadn't taken his eyes off of Anna—leaned

closer to her. "I'm sorry—I didn't catch that. What did you say?"

Anna made a face. "Continue," she said, reluctantly.

Alex leaned back. "Good. Now, where was I?"

"You were at the part where you figured out I didn't own any pets," Anna said sarcastically.

"Aaanna," Alex warned.

Anna put on a face of innocence. "I was just trying to be helpful."

Alex gave her one last look and then continued. "So, we know that no one but you and your mom live in your house and therefore, whatever or whoever was in your room was not someone you live with."

"Brilliant deduction, Alex," Anna said, stifling a yawn.

Alex ignored her and turned a page in his notebook. "Within the last week, three of your favorite items went missing—your pink fuzzy feather pen, your purple and pink striped locking diary that doesn't lock anymore, and your Falling Awake book. You searched high and low and could not find them anywhere." He looked closer at his notes. "You even checked your closet," he added, circling something in his notebook, "thoroughly."

Anna gave Alex a look. "Yes," she drawled.

Alex licked his thumb and turned another page in his notebook. "That brings us to last night. At roughly nine o'clock you were laying in your bed *listening* for a clue as to what was going on in your room."

Anna massaged her temples. "Alex, I really don't get how this is helping."

"See, this part—this part is kind of peculiar," Alex said tapping his pencil on his notebook.

Anna perked up. "What part?" She leaned forward to try and see what Alex had written in his notes. Alex pulled his notebook closer to his chest.

"Listening?" he said. "Why on earth were you listening and what were you listening for?"

Anna leaned back. "Oh, geez, this again," she mumbled. "I really don't know how many more times I can tell you this." Anna opened her eyes wide and spoke painfully slow. "I... don't... know."

Alex considered Anna's reply and then made a clicking sound in his mouth. "Yah, I know you keep saying that, but I don't buy it."

Anna threw her hands up. "You don't *buy* it?" she said, incredulous. "He doesn't buy it," she said to her ceiling. She looked back at Alex. "Do you think I am lying?"

"Nope," Alex said, matter-of-factly.

"Then why do you keep saying," Anna imitated his voice, "'I don't buy it'?"

Alex smiled. "I... don't... know," he replied. His smile widened. "But it's peculiar."

Anna slapped her forehead and Alex continued.

"Okay, so after you *listened,* you heard a rustling noise coming from the closet. You decided it was a mouse so you grabbed your bat and went to the closet to kill the mouse."

"I didn't plan on *killing* the mouse," Anna said defensively.

Alex looked up from his notes. "Anna, mice are this big," he spread two fingers out about three inches, "and your bat is this big," he threw his arms out as wide as they would go. What did you think would happen when you hit the small mouse with your large bat?"

"I don't know," Anna shot back, flustered. "I wasn't thinking—I was scared."

"Of a mouse?" Alex asked, unconvinced.

"No!" Anna yelled. "Of whatever was in the closet. I was *hoping* it was a mouse, but it sounded too big to be a mouse and I was scared, okay?" Anna cradled her knees to her chest. "I'm not perfect, you know," she added.

"Don't worry," Alex smirked, "I am well aware of that."

Anna reached over and shoved him. Alex chuckled and turned to the next page of his notes.

"Okay," Alex said, regaining his composure, "so there you are with your enormous bat about to *injure* a poor defenseless mouse—that had a thing for fuzzy feather pens, broken locking diaries, and books on Dream Traveling—"

"Aaalex?" Anna warned.

Alex hid a smile. "I'm just going through the facts."

Anna shoved him again and Alex laughed. "Okay, sorry. You opened the closet door and you saw a boy. It says the boy was sitting down, he had all your things with him, and right before he disappeared, he said he wanted to learn how to fall awake. You *do* remember that he looked about eight years old and he had blonde hair. You *don't* remember whether his hair was long or short, what clothes he had on, whether he spoke in an accent, or if he used your name when he talked to you." Alex made another clicking sound in his mouth. "Oh, and you don't remember if the pen, diary, and book floated back down to the ground or fell to the ground—or how they ended up on the ground."

Anna had been picking mindlessly at a hole in her jeans when she felt Alex staring at her. She looked up and met his stare. "What?" she said, innocently.

Alex looked down at this notes and rubbed his chin. "This last part—it really seals the deal for me."

Anna stopped picking at her jeans. "Last part?" she asked. "Seals what deal?"

"You don't remember any crucial details about the boy, but you do remember that as soon as the boy disappeared, you—and I quote—'woke up' in your bed." Alex shrugged. "If you woke up, then you must have been asleep. And if you were asleep, there is a good chance you were dreaming or—more specifically—Dream Traveling."

"I- I—" Anna stuttered.

"Yes?" Alex said calmly.

"I didn't say I woke up. I said I was back in my bed."

"Nope." Alex shook his head. "You said you 'woke up'. And besides, how would you—in an instant—go from your closet door to your bed?"

"I didn't say I woke up!" Anna yelled. "And I could have like blacked out going back to my bed from fear or something. I wasn't dreaming. I mean, I never fell asleep. You can't dream if you're not asleep—right?"

Alex considered Anna's question for a long moment, and then he looked down at his notes, rubbed at his chin, and slowly stood up. "Are you sure you don't remember anything more about the boy? Did he look familiar to you? Did he seem upset or in trouble of some kind?"

Anna let out an exasperated scream and buried her head in her knees. "I'm dying here!" she yelled, her head still tucked downward.

Alex—who had begun pacing again—suddenly stopped and shot Anna a look of startled surprise. "Wait, what did you just say?" he asked, urgently.

Anna's head sprang up to reveal her face contorted in a dramatic display of anguish. "You're killing me!" she yelled. "It's Saturday and I have spent my entire morning sitting in the same room, in the same spot, answering the same questions over and over. Face it—we're not going to figure out who or what—"

Alex put up a quick hand to interrupt Anna and then

took a step closer to her. "No, not that. What did you say first?"

"Huh?" Anna threw her hands up. "What are you talking about?"

"When you first screamed—what did you say to me?"

Anna rolled her eyes towards the ceiling and then back down to Alex. "I am dying here," she said, exaggerating each word. She was about to launch into a tirade about her numb legs, his repetitive questions, and their obvious inability to solve the mystery when she caught his face. Alex was beaming. His reaction caught her off guard.

"What?" she asked, her face softening.

He jumped forward and kissed her quickly on the cheek. "You're brilliant," he chirped.

"I'm... I'm..." Anna touched her check. "I'm what? What are you talking about?"

Alex smiled wide. "You just figured out the secret to your mystery boy."

Chapter 3

Brothers

It would be a long walk back to the house from the fields—close to two miles Morgan figured. He leaned against his plow—weary to the bone—and eyed with dread the two large bundles that sat near his feet. *A long walk indeed,* he thought, *especially with such a heavy load.*

Morgan wiped his damp forehead and then turned and looked in the direction of the setting sun. In less than an hour it would be black as pitch and cold. Already the air had a bite to it. Morgan pulled at his threadbare coat searching for warmth between the holes and tears. With another wipe of his brow and a heavy sigh, he leaned down and grabbed the two over-stuffed sacks filled with corn and rolled them both onto his back. He wobbled under their weight, struggling to find his balance, and then he steadied his footing. Taking short, wide steps, Morgan began his slow trek home.

It had been like this almost every day for close to a month—ever since his father had joined the militia to fight against the French. It was his duty as a man, his father had argued, and what an argument it had been. Morgan and his brother weren't supposed to have heard it, but in a two room cabin in the quiet of the late night, it was hard listening to much else.

Morgan had kept a tight hand over his brother's mouth so he could be sure to hear every word. Morgan was only nine years old, but he was smart enough to know that the outcome of that argument would immediately affect his world. When his mother had begun pleading and then crying, Morgan knew she was fighting a losing battle. His father hated any display of emotion—he found it weak and (in his own words) "unnecessary".

"Who will tend the fields while you are gone?" his mother cried. "Surely, you can't expect Charlie to."

Morgan couldn't see his father's face, but he knew without looking that his father had scowled at his mother's comment. The silence after she had spoken was louder than a musket shot.

Charlie squirmed under the weight of Morgan's hand. Morgan pressed a finger to his lips and Charlie—thinking they were playing a game—silently clapped his big, meaty hands together. Morgan stroked his brother's arm with his free hand and waited for more news.

"Morgan," his father finally replied. Being a man of few words, it was all he would say, but Morgan knew what his father meant. Morgan would be expected to fill his father's shoes.

"But he is just a boy," his mother argued, "and what about Charlie? Morgan is all he has. It will break his heart to be separated from him."

"We all have to sacrifice in times of war," his father responded coldly. "Besides, it's time they both grew up."

"But you know as well as I do that Charlie isn't capable of—"

"That's enough, woman," his father barked. "I've made up my mind. I leave in the morning."

Morgan could hear his mother crying again. "When will you return?" she said trying—without success—to control herself. "What if something happens to you?"

Morgan never heard his father reply. Instead, he fell asleep to the fitful crying of his mother and Charlie's light snores.

The next morning had been a blur of activity and haste as his father rushed to pack his few essentials and prepare Morgan for his new role as head of the house. Charlie, as innocent as a small child, shadowed Morgan and their father around the cabin and then out to the fields.

"He's not to come with you when you go to work the fields, do you understand me?" Morgan's father spoke sternly and he refused to look at Charlie.

But even Charlie knew his father was talking about him. His large, husky body visibly shrank under the weight of his father's command. It broke Morgan's heart to see that Charlie understood that they would not be able to be together as much. To lessen the blow, Morgan slid a sly hand over to Charlie and squeezed his brother's thick arm in loving reassurance. Instantly, Charlie brightened. He even did a little skip in the air.

Had their father not been so preoccupied with his departure, he would have punished them both for what he would have termed "disobedient disrespect" for his authority. But as it was, he either didn't notice or didn't care. Less than thirty minutes later, he was gone. It would be the last time either of them would see their father.

Morgan was getting closer to home—he knew because he could see light from the cabin. His mother, worried for her young son's safety, had made a habit of lighting candles for him and setting them in the front two windows. It was an expense Morgan knew would have greatly upset his father. That fact made him smile in spite of his fatigue.

Morgan walked more quickly now that he knew his day was coming to an end. At any moment, he would be spotted by Charlie who waited like an eager puppy at the front door of their cabin for his best friend—his brother—to come home. His mother reported that Charlie took his position sometimes as early as lunch—waiting and watching for Morgan to come back. As soon as Charlie spotted Morgan slowly dawdling over the ridge, he would begin screaming Morgan's name. It always made Morgan laugh, no matter how tired he was.

And this night was no different. Charlie was outside chanting Morgan's name into the darkness and dancing around in anticipation of his brother's arrival home. The soft glow from the candles in the cabin's windows lit his performance. Morgan adjusted his grip on the heavy sacks and quickened his pace. He had missed Charlie, too.

At six feet tall, Charlie was a giant even compared to adults. But he was a gentle giant. His mother described him as a sixteen-year-old five-year-old. Others referred to him as "special" adding raised eyebrows or sympathetic nods to their assessment. Morgan's mother would ignore their gestures and simply say in response, "Yes, he is special," her face beaming with pride. She loved him with the fierce protectiveness of a mother bear.

Morgan's father, on the other hand, did not share his mother's opinion. To him, Charlie was a constant reminder of his failure to produce a normal child. And to make matters worse, Charlie was the spitting image of his father—thick black hair, fair skin, and the palest blue eyes one could imagine. He had been a beautiful baby and a handsome boy, but once Charlie was past his toddler years it became clear to everyone, including his father, that he was not like other kids. It was then that Charlie's father began to distance himself from his son—refusing to take him into town or to be seen with him.

From stories Morgan had overheard and comments his mother had made, Morgan had pieced together that, before he was born, Charlie had been all but invisible to his father and completely isolated from the outside world. The thought of how that must have hurt Charlie pained Morgan to the point of tears each time he considered it. It meant that for seven years, Charlie had been alone except for the love his mother secretly shined on him when his father was in the fields or in town. His father forbade any show of emotion toward Charlie claiming that it would make Charlie's "condition" worse.

And so it was not surprising that when Morgan was born, the lonely young Charlie looked upon the new baby as an incredible gift, showering him with attention and treating him as though he were a most prized possession. He loved Morgan so much that his mother feared his heart would burst from joy. And Morgan, every bit his mother's son down to his wavy blonde hair, big brown eyes, and small build, idolized his big brother, copying his clumsy walk, his boisterous laugh, and his innocent pranks.

It wasn't until he was about six years old and Charlie was thirteen that Morgan began to realize his brother was slower than other kids the same age. Charlie still sucked his thumb and he was never allowed to join their father in the fields or even go to school. Morgan found out later that his mother had sent Charlie to school when he was younger, convinced that an education and being around other kids would help him improve, but Charlie had lasted less than two weeks. Every day he had come home crying, complaining that the other kids were teasing him. When he'd come home one day with blood running down his face and a large knot on his head (one of the kids at school had thrown a rock at him), his mother told Charlie he didn't have to go back.

When it was time for Morgan to go to school, it was heartbreaking leaving his big brother. He felt so bad that Charlie couldn't come with him that, instead of hanging around after school to play with the other kids, Morgan rushed home to share all he had learned with Charlie. It was the highlight of the day for them both.

It was then that Morgan and Charlie's relationship had begun to change. As Morgan began to mature, instead of idolizing his brother he felt increasingly protective of him. Charlie was slow, but he wasn't stupid. He was painfully aware that he was different and it hurt him deeply to made fun of or—worse—to be ignored. Knowing that, Morgan felt it was his duty to protect his brother's heart from the cruelty of others—most especially their father. He took care never to speak harshly to Charlie or to lose his patience with him. And Morgan constantly reminded Charlie of how smart he was and how much he loved him.

When others were not as kind to Charlie, Morgan was

as valiant as a knight in his efforts to defend his older brother. He'd even stood up to their father once when their father—in a fit of anger—had told their mother, while Morgan and Charlie looked on, that he wished Charlie had never been born. Reacting out of instinct, Morgan had yelled back at his father, saying that his comment showed what a fool he was because Charlie was the best thing about their family. His father had struck him so hard that Morgan wore a bruise on his face for weeks. It was also the only time Morgan had ever seen Charlie cry.

After that, Morgan had never talked back to his father again. Instead, he protected his brother by showering him with more love and attention. His displays of affection greatly irritated their father and it often earned Morgan more chores, but he didn't care. Charlie had never been happier.

Morgan was close enough to the cabin now to see Charlie's face, and once they locked eyes, he rushed to Morgan, grabbed the heavy sacks off his back, and threw them over his own back as though they were as light as feathers. His face beaming, Charlie patted Morgan's back repeating over and over, "Morgan home. Morgan home."

Morgan, weary but relieved his day was over, smiled and echoed back, "Yes, Morgan home. Morgan home."

"Morgan?" their mother called from inside the cabin. "Hurry in son. You'll catch your death of cold and your dinner is ready."

Charlie raced inside the house in front of his brother, dropped the sacks of corn inside the front door, and made for the kitchen table. Morgan followed slowly behind him, feeling every step. When Charlie got to the table, he pulled out Morgan's chair and pointed excitedly to a bowl set in his place. Both Morgan and his mother laughed.

When Morgan made it to the table and sat down, he looked into the small bowl and saw watery soup. He stared at the soup—silent.

"Go ahead, son," said his mother. "Charlie and I have already eaten. And don't worry, I have enough for you to have seconds."

Morgan forced a smile and scooped up a small spoon of the bland looking soup. Slowly, he poured the soup back into the bowl.

"Is there any bread?" he asked, hopeful.

Charlie smiled wide and giggled. "No bread," he sang, "just water soup." Then he began dancing in place and humming to himself.

Morgan's face sagged.

"It's not water," his mother said putting a hand on Charlie's back to calm him. "There is some corn in there and a bit of cabbage."

Morgan sighed and then, slowly, he began slurping down the soup. It was the fifth day in a row they had eaten the same soup. And breakfast was not much better—a few eggs and maybe a corn pancake. Since their father had left it had become increasingly hard to manage the farm and the fields. Much of their small crop went to pay for their land and a smaller portion was used to feed their milk cow and their chickens. Any leftovers were used in town to trade for other food and supplies. But there hadn't been leftovers lately. In fact, there had barely been enough to feed the cow and chickens.

Charlie sat down next to Morgan at the kitchen table and watched as he ate. Charlie was smiling as though he was hiding a big secret. Morgan, exhausted, didn't notice. Charlie leaned in closer, hoping Morgan would look up. But Morgan continued the slow drain of his soup, his mind lost in thought. Charlie, feeling as though he might explode, finally screamed, "Ask me!"

Morgan looked up. Charlie was hoping up and down in his chair—a wide smile plastered across his face.

"Charlie," his mother warned. She was sitting in a chair nearby, mending one of Morgan's socks. There was an unfamiliar edge to her voice and it caught Morgan's attention.

"Ask me!" Charlie screamed again, laughing and clapping his big hands together.

"Charlie!" his mother yelled and she stood up from her chair, her face flushed with—was it fear or anger? Morgan couldn't decide, but he had a funny feeling in the pit of his stomach. He put a hand out to his brother to calm him.

"Okay, Charlie," Morgan soothed. "Okay. What is it?"

"Guess!" Charlie said. He clasped his own hand across his mouth and stifled a giggle.

Morgan looked at his mother. She was still standing in front of her chair, his sock in her hand and her face white. She seemed frozen in place.

"Mother?" Morgan asked. But before she could explain, Charlie grabbed Morgan's face and turned it back towards him.

"Mother is leaving tomorrow to find Father, and I get to be with you all day long in the fields!" He practically jumped out of his chair with excitement.

Morgan's mother drifted slowly back down into her chair, the sock still in her hand. She refused to make eye contact with Morgan.

"Mother," Morgan asked, his head swimming, "what's Charlie talking about?" Charlie patted his brother's hand excitedly.

"Every day!" Charlie squealed. "Every day!" he whispered.

Morgan smiled at Charlie. "That's... that's great, Charlie. Mother," he asked again, "what's going on?"

"Morgan," his mother began, tears rolling down her cheeks, "we can't keep going on like this. We need your father back."

Charlie was clapping his hands together. Morgan reached out and stopped his hands and Charlie's expression dimmed.

"We don't need him," Morgan said, his voiced laced with anger. "We never needed him."

As hard as the last month had been, it was also the first time there had been a sense of peace in the house. They all laughed more, talked more—they even exchanged hugs and kisses on cheeks before bed. It was strange, but without their father around, it finally felt like they were a real family. If their father returned now, all that would end.

Morgan's mother looked down at her lap, and then back to her son. "We do need him, Morgan. You've done a great job, but you're just a young boy. It was foolish to think you could do the work of your father. And we are suffering. How many more days do you think we can live on water soup, eggs, and corn pancakes?" She wiped her tears with Morgan's sock.

"It's not that bad, Mother," Morgan insisted. "And besides, I can work harder. And... and Charlie can help me. He's strong."

"I am very strong," Charlie agreed, proudly.

"Morgan, it won't be enough. Our only chance is to find your father and bring him back."

"But that's crazy!" Morgan shot back. "Even if you could find him, you know he would never come back—not while the war is going on."

Morgan's mother got up slowly from her chair and walked to the kitchen table. Morgan looked up into her eyes and—for the first time—saw how scared she was. The fear he saw made him nauseous and he pushed away his half eaten bowl of soup.

His mother reached into the pocket of her dress and pulled out a folded piece of paper.

"I found this in town today." She unfolded the paper and put on the table in front of Morgan.

Charlie—whom Morgan was teaching to read—jumped up from the table. "Me!" he screamed. "Me! Me! Me! I want to read!"

But Morgan could already see the top line. *Local Militia in nearby Crown Point. Supplies needed.*

"Read it," said Morgan's mother softly. "It says they think the war may be over soon. They may even be releasing some of the militia."

Charlie reached down and picked up the paper, bringing it close to his face.

Morgan looked up at his mother. "He won't come back," he said quietly. "Even if they let some of the soldiers go, he'll fight to stay until it's over."

"Maybe," his mother said, wiping at a tear that had escaped down her cheek, "but maybe when he sees me and he hears how hard it's been for us, he'll come back. We need him," she said again.

"Where is Crown Point?" Charlie asked, proud that he could read the words.

"Far," Morgan said. Slowly he pulled his soup back.

Morgan's mother bit her bottom lip and fought the urge to cry. Her plan was risky. She knew that. And it meant that Morgan would have to shoulder even more responsibility while she was away and that caused her great worry. But if she didn't try to bring their father back, she feared her children would suffer starvation or sickness. Worse, she feared they would die from it.

Putting on a bright face of enthusiasm, she turned to Charlie and patted his back. "Crown Point isn't that far," she said happily. "I'll be gone a week or two at the most. And while I am gone, you and Morgan will be the men of the house."

"The men of the house!" Charlie cheered. He bent down to Morgan and raised his eyebrows in joy. He mouthed the words *men of the house* and clapped his hands together.

"You boys will work the fields together," their mother continued, "and feed the cow and chickens, chop the wood—"

"I chop wood really good!" Charlie interrupted.

"Yes, you do," agreed his mother. "And you'll have to cook the meals, make your beds, and take baths in the river."

Charlie scowled, "No baths," he said, folding his arms across his chest and pouting.

Morgan had stopped listening. Instead he was lost in his own thoughts. His mother was right. He wasn't able to work the fields as well as his father. And they were suffering.

He knew that. Every night he went to bed listening to the growling of his own stomach.

But it wasn't just his age and his size that was preventing him from matching his father's labor. His heart just wasn't in it. He daydreamed all the time. Where he really wanted to be was at school—learning. There was a great big world outside of their cabin and, more than anything, Morgan wanted to experience that world. So if his father did come back, it would mean he would get to go back to school. But what kind of family would they be with their father back? It would be hard for all of them—but especially for Charlie. And then a most horrible thought came to Morgan.

"Mother?" Morgan asked, interrupting what looked to be a jig she was doing with Charlie. She continued dancing, unaware that Morgan was calling for her. "Mother?" Morgan repeated, his voice tight with concern. She looked up at him as she continued to jump up and down with Charlie. "What happens if you don't come back?" Morgan asked his face stretched tight with worry.

Morgan's mother threw her head back and laughed as if that was the most ridiculous thing she had ever heard. "Only death and the devil could keep me from my boys," she said twirling Charlie in a circle.

It was a strange feeling and Morgan didn't know why, but for some reason he had to fight the urge to cry.

Chapter 4

Wide Awake

"Aaa... aaa... Aaalex." Anna was stuttering, and her face had suddenly turned the color of gray sky.

Alex, confused, took a step closer to her. "Anna, is it something I said?"

Anna scooted back violently and raised a shaky finger towards her closet, but before Alex could turn around, the room was lit with bright yellow-orange light, as if the sun itself were setting in Anna's room.

Anna screamed once as her closet door exploded open, and Alex was pushed forward onto the carpet next to her. Before either of them could make sense of what had just happened, the sound of deep, rich, hearty laughter filled the small space of Anna's room.

Anna—who'd been hiding her head between her knees—looked up. Filling the doorway of her closet and haloed by the same yellow-orange light that now lit her room, was the head of—

"Mama Do-Right!" Alex yelled. He was so surprised to see her and to see only her head that he couldn't complete a thought. "What? Why? What's going? I mean – wow! This is amazing!"

Anna, surprisingly, was very calm. "So the boy in the closet *is* my assignment?" she asked, almost hoping she was wrong, and not just because she didn't want Alex to be right. She still didn't understand how it could be possible, since she was almost positive she hadn't been dreaming when she saw the boy.

Mama Do-Right smiled and then laughed at both Alex and Anna. "Don't I get a 'hello' or 'how are you'? It has been a bit of time," she giggled, "since we last saw each other." And then she winked at Anna. "Anything is possible, my child, or have you already forgotten the most important lesson of all?"

Alex looked between Anna and Mama Do-Right, confused. "Did I miss something?"

Anna ignored Alex and repeated her question. "So the boy *is* my assignment—is that what you are saying?"

Alex reached for his notebook, which had fallen on the floor when he was pushed down, and grabbed for his pencil. Mama Do-Right considered Anna's question and then smiled.

"Yes," she said, confidently.

Alex raised his hand in a cheer. "I told you so," he whispered to Anna. Anna stuck her tongue out at him.

"And, no," Mama Do-Right added.

"What?" Anna and Alex said in unison, both turning to look at her.

Mama Do-Right's face shimmered and glowed and she laughed again. "Well, this is all my fault," she said, apologetically.

"What's all your fault?" Anna asked.

"Yah," Alex said, opening his notebook. He flipped rapidly thru his notes until he found a blank page. "What is your fault?" he added, his pencil ready to jot down her response.

Mama Do-Right hesitated. "There are some missing pages from the Falling Awake book."

Anna and Alex exchanged looks. "How many pages?" Anna asked slowly.

"Yah," Alex said, "how many pages?" He pressed his pencil to the paper of his notebook, waiting for Mama Do-Right's answer.

"Well," Mama Do-Right cast her eyes upward as though she was struggling to remember and then she looked back at Alex and Anna. "I know—for sure—the section about how you don't have to be sleeping to be dreaming is missing." She smiled and winked at Anna.

"An entire section?" Alex echoed in disbelief. "How is that possible?"

Mama Do-Right looked as if she was about to answer Alex as Anna cut her off.

"Wait, that isn't even the right question to be asking right now. What do you mean I don't have to be sleeping to be dreaming? And who was the boy in my closet? Is he an assignment or isn't he?"

"Anna, she already answered your last question," Alex said, matter-of-factly. "And it is kind of a big deal that we're missing a section of the Falling Awake—"

"She didn't answer the question," Anna said, heatedly, cutting Alex off. "Yes and no? That isn't an answer—it's a riddle. And I think knowing more about the boy in my closet is a lot more important right now than the Falling Awake book." She crossed her arms on her chest and gave Alex a defiant look.

Alex shrugged. "Which came first," he asked, "the chicken or the egg?"

Anna rolled her eyes and threw her hands up. "Which came first—the chicken or the egg? What in the world does that mean? Do you see what I have to put up with?" Anna looked back at her closet for Mama Do-Right's face, but Mama Do-Right was gone.

"Mama Do-Right?" Anna said, hesitantly.

"Mama Do-Right?" Alex repeated.

The closet was still glowing bright yellow-orange but there was no sign of Mama Do-Right.

"I hate it when she does this," Anna whispered under

her breath.

"Does what?' Alex asked, not taking his eyes off the closet.

"Disappears," Anna said dryly. "C'mon."

Alex turned and looked at Anna. "C'mon what?" he asked.

Anna was already on her feet. "We're on assignment." She reached her hand back to Alex. "I can't do it without you," she said, her face softening.

Alex looked up at Anna and then back at the closet. "We're going in there?" he asked.

"Yup," she said.

"And we're not dreaming," Alex said, trying to confirm their state.

Anna sighed. "That part I don't know yet. But I am pretty sure the answer to that question lies somewhere in that closet." She bent over and grabbed Alex's hand. "C'mon," she said again.

Alex took Anna's hand and she pulled him up. He stowed his pencil back behind his ear, folded his notebook in half, and shoved it into his back pocket. "You know, Anna, you are probably the bravest person I know." He gave her a shy smile.

Anna took his hand again and began pulling him towards the closet door. "Thanks, Alex. And I'm sorry I said your questions were stupid." They stopped in front of the closet. And then Anna remembered. "Wait, right before Mama Do-Right showed up, you said something about me figuring out the mystery of the boy."

Alex's face brightened. "Yes! The boy, Anna. He's dead." Alex smiled wide.

"What?" Anna looked horrified. "What do you mean he's dead?"

Alex shook his head. "No, not he's dead because we didn't help him. He's dead—meaning he is a ghost. Your assignment. He's a ghost!"

And at that moment, Anna and Alex disappeared into the yellow-orange light of the closet.

It was still dark outside and already it was early morning. Morgan knew that because the roosters had crowed and the air smelled sweet from the dew on the grass. He had slept all night with the window shutters open. He told himself, and his brother, that he wanted them open in case he woke in the middle of the night and was able to catch a glimpse of the stars. But in his heart, he knew the real reason he had left the window open was to be sure he heard his mother leave on her journey to find his father.

Morgan hadn't yet sat up in bed. He was worried that his movement might wake Charlie. And as much as he loved his older brother, he had few truly peaceful moments to himself. And so he lay in his small single bed, facing his open window, and watched as the morning crawled to its wake and greeted the day. When the first haze of yellow light began rising on the horizon, Morgan heard the light patter of his mother's feet downstairs.

Their home was only a one-bedroom cabin, but after his mother had given birth to Charlie, their father had built a make-shift loft over the living area and the main bedroom. Luckily, Morgan's father had also seen fit to build a window. It turned what could have been a very dark space into a cozy hideaway with a view. The window was Morgan's favorite part of the cabin.

Down below, Morgan's mother was busy. He could hear her making quick paths between her bedroom and the kitchen area. Morgan closed his eyes and took a deep breath. *Should I go down and help her?* he thought reluctantly, not wanting to leave the coziness of his bed, but mostly not wanting to accept that morning had come and that his mother was, indeed, leaving. Just the thought of it brought tears to his eyes.

The night before he had—after much coaxing from his mother and Charlie—danced in the living room. Then his mother and Charlie stayed up late listening to him as he read out loud—to Charlie's delight. It was a similar night to many others they had shared since their father had left. *Maybe,* he reasoned, *this is the cause of my tears.* Maybe he feared the return of his father and the end of their family joy and this was causing him great sadness. Morgan tried that thought on for size, trying to determine if it explained the overwhelming sadness he felt. But after a moment's consideration, he shook his head. There was no doubt that once his father came back (*if* his father came back, he corrected), the joyful nights would disappear and that thought *was* disappointing. But the sadness he was feeling was much deeper.

There was banging in the kitchen. It sounded as if his mother was making them breakfast before she left. Morgan wiped at a tear that had spilled down his cheek. The sadness he felt had to do with his mother. As Morgan unveiled the truth to himself, a crushing heaviness fell over him. He didn't want his mother to go. And of course, he would miss her greatly while she was away—but there was something else eating at him from the dark corners of his thoughts. He just couldn't shake the feeling that if his mother left, he would never see her again.

Morgan twisted uncomfortably under the heavy thickness of his blankets. The noise caused Charlie to stir. Immediately, Morgan stopped and waited to see if his restlessness had woken his brother. But when Charlie's light snoring resumed, Morgan breathed a sigh of relief.

There's nothing to worry about, Morgan told himself. His mother had told him the exact same words the night before when she noticed the concern on Morgan's face. "It's a short journey," she'd added, patting his small shoulder. "I will be back before you know it." But her comments had little effect on him. And now—with her departure at hand—his feeling of unease was increasing in intensity with each passing moment.

Go down and beg her not to go, he ordered himself. But he knew that would be pointless. His mother was almost as stubborn as his father. When she got an idea in her head, it was near impossible to stop her. *You could at least try,* he argued with himself. Morgan hid his face behind his small, calloused hands. "Stop," he whispered.

Before he could think of much else, he heard small footsteps on the stairs leading up to the loft. As Morgan lowered his hands from his face, he found the sweet face of his mother staring back at him. She smiled lovingly. Morgan had to fight the urge not to cry.

As quiet as a cat, his mother made her way over to him and sat down on the edge of his bed. Morgan forced a weak smile. She reached out her hand and stroked the side of his face. It broke her heart to see the fear in his eyes. She turned her face away from him—pretending she was looking over at Charlie in the bed across the small room—but in truth, she was hiding her own face so that Morgan would not see her own concern or sadness.

Morgan sat up and took his mother's hand in his. "Don't go," he whispered. "Please."

His mother turned back around—her face composed. She wrapped her arms around Morgan's tiny shoulders and held him close.

"What I am doing," she whispered into his ear, "I do for

all of us. You belong in school and your father belongs in the fields."

Morgan pulled back and stared down at his blankets. "And Charlie?" he asked, looking back up at his mother. "What happens to Charlie if Father returns?"

His mother raised her eyebrows. "*If* Father returns?" she repeated. "You mean, *when* Father returns."

Morgan looked back down.

"Charlie has the spirit of an angel," she whispered and smiled. "He will be just fine."

Morgan's throat tightened and he fought back tears. "And you?" he said quietly.

Morgan's mother slowly patted her son's hand. "I am as strong as a bull." And then she winked.

Morgan nodded slowly glancing at Charlie who—surprisingly—was still sleeping deeply. When he looked back at his mother, he saw tears in her eyes. He tightened his grip on her hand and questioned her with his eyes.

She shrugged off his concern and pulled him in for another hug. "I am so proud of you," she whispered. "You are the most incredible son and the best brother." He heard her sniff a few times. "I am going to miss our dances and your book readings." Then she pulled back quickly.

"I have made you breakfast downstairs," she continued, as if nothing was out of the ordinary. "And there should be enough grain, potatoes, and corn to last you for at least ten days. Have Charlie milk the cow tomorrow and keep the chickens fed."

Morgan knew the moment he had been dreading was upon them. With a light pat on his blanketed leg, his mother stood and smoothed down the front of her dress. "Be good to each other," she whispered and blew Morgan a kiss. When she made to turn and leave, Morgan reached up and grabbed her hand.

"Aren't you going to say goodbye to Charlie?" he asked.

His mother stole a look at her oldest son sleeping like a baby in his bed and she shook her head. "No," she said. "Let him sleep. I will give him a big hug when I return with your father." She patted Morgan's hand and reluctantly he released his hold on her. "I'll be seeing you," she added and smiled.

Morgan forced a smile and then watched as she made her way quietly back down the stairs. When he heard the front door of the cabin open, his heart sank. And when the front door closed, Charlie woke wearing a big, wide smile.

"It's just the two of us now!" he said excitedly, his hair bushy, his face puffy, and his voice rough from a long night of sleep.

"Yes, Charlie," Morgan agreed, staring again out their window. He watched his mother's small frame grow smaller and smaller as she walked down the path that lead away from their cabin. "It's just us now," he echoed.

Chapter Five

On the Road

"Who turned off the light?" Alex hissed, squirming next to Anna.

Almost as soon as they'd stepped into the yellow-orange light of Anna's closet, both Alex and Anna had found themselves in the dark. That alone was unnerving, but it also felt like they were trapped in a small space.

"How do we get out of here?" Anna asked, feeling along the walls that surrounded them.

Alex ignored Anna's question and continued to twist and turn, pushing and shoving up against her.

"Alex!" Anna yelled. "Cut it out! Spazzing out in here is not going to help anything," she added, annoyed.

"I can't breathe," Alex said breathlessly. "I'm not good in small, dark spaces—seriously."

Anna turned in the direction of his voice. "What?" she

asked. "Since when?"

Alex was sweating now and checking his own pulse. "Since ever," he said weakly.

"Wow—that's, like, really weird because I have known you your whole life and I never—"

"Anna!" Alex barked. "Just figure out if there is a way out of here."

"Okay, okay," she shot back, "keep your pants on." Anna ran her hand along the walls again. "It's some kind of wood or something." Her hand caught on a snag. "Ouch," she winced. "Rough wood," she added, sucking on her wound.

"Anna," Alex begged, "hurry!"

Anna reached her hand out again and almost immediately felt a seam in the wood. "Aha!" she yelled. "Gotcha." She ran her hand up the seam and hit what felt like a small metal square. She fumbled around clumsily, trying to see if she could find a latch of some kind, but there was nothing.

"Alex, bad news."

"What?" he said, his breathing shallow.

"I think we are locked in some kind of tall box."

"Tall box?" he moaned. "Great," he whispered.

"Maybe I can break it open, though." Anna crouched back as if she was going to jump forward.

"Wait!" Alex screamed.

But it was too late. Anna threw all her weight against

the seam she had found and, almost instantly, the tall box fell forward, taking Anna and Alex with it.

Alex was near hysterics. "You've trapped us!" He struggled to turn himself around in the box so he was not facing what was now the bottom of the tall box.

Anna—dazed from their fall—took a moment to register Alex's comment. "What are you talking about?" Anna twisted around until she, too, was not facing downward.

"You tipped the box forward and now we've landed on the front of it." Alex banged a frustrated hand against one of the walls. "We've landed on the opening of the box!" he added dramatically.

"Oh no," Anna said now, realizing what she had done. "So the door to the tall box..."

"Is under us," Alex said, completing her sentence.

Anna rubbed her chin.

"Mama Do-Right!" Alex screamed. "Mama Do-Right!"

"If I were you, I'd save my energy," Anna said calmly.

"Anna, I *have* to get out of here," Alex squeaked. "Mama Do-Right is our only hope at this point."

"Not quite," Anna said.

"Not quite? How else are we going to get out of here—I don't have an axe, do you?"

Anna's face lit up. "Alex, you're brilliant!"

Alex moaned. "I could have told you that, but my brilliance is not going to help us now that we are trapped in a dark box with no way out."

If there had been light in the box, Alex would have been able to see almost instantly that Anna wasn't listening to a word he was saying. She was too busy concentrating on imagining an axe in her hand.

"Anna?" Alex said into the dark when Anna didn't respond.

Anna laughed and then reached out, feeling for Alex's hand. "Here," she said.

Alex's fingers wrapped around what felt to be a thick wooden handle. "What's this?" he asked, surprised.

Anna let go of it and Alex's hand dropped back weighed down by an—

"It's an axe," Anna said proudly.

"An axe?" said Alex, dumbfounded. He slid his free hand up the long handle until he felt the cold metal of the axe's blade. "How did you..." he whispered, his voice fading as he struggled to digest how Anna had created an axe out of thin air.

"We're dreaming, so I just imagined an axe and it appeared." Anna was beaming.

"But-but—," Alex stammered, "we're not dreaming—I mean, we weren't dreaming in your bedroom and then we walked into your closet and landed here and..." He paused, confused. "We're *not* dreaming, right?"

Anna smiled in the dark. "Well, that's what I thought, too, until I imagined the axe and it appeared."

Alex, suddenly remembering they were still in the

cramped tall box, started breathing hard again and sweating. "Okay, Anna," he wheezed, "whatever you say, just take the axe and get us out of here."

Anna's smile dimmed. "Me?" she said. "I don't know how to use an axe. Besides, I can barely lift it."

"Anna," Alex panted, "I am in no shape to use the axe. You're going to have to do it."

Anna groaned.

"Please, Anna," Alex begged.

She took a deep breath. "Fine. But I can't make any promises."

Alex nodded, forgetting Anna couldn't see him in the dark box.

Anna reached over and felt for the axe. Alex had it leaning against his leg. Gently she pulled the axe towards her.

"Hurry," Alex whined.

"Okay, okay, okay," Anna said, quickly. She reached down, wrapped her small hands around the wooden handle, and made to pick up the axe. Then she stopped and straightened up. "Wait a minute," she said, excitedly.

"What?" Alex said impatiently.

Anna pressed her hands on either side of her forehead and pinched her eyes closed. Within seconds, the box they were in tilted back upwards to its original position.

"Whoa!" Alex screamed as their bodies bounced against the back of the box.

Before Alex could gather his thoughts and ask Anna what had just happened, he heard a clicking noise at the front of the box. He turned around as the front of the box opened to reveal a small, darkened cabin bedroom.

Alex screamed in surprise and Anna squealed and clapped her hands together. "It worked," she chirped.

Alex slowly turned his head towards her, his face slack in disbelief. "What did you do?" he whispered.

"If I could imagine an axe, I could imagine the box tipping back and unlocking." Anna stepped out of the box, proudly offering a hand to Alex.

Now that she was out of the box she could see clearly what they had been trapped in. And it wasn't a box—well, not really.

"It's a wardrobe," Alex said, the color coming back to his face now that he was out of the cramped dark place.

"A wardrobe?" Anna echoed.

"Yah, it's like a closet. You hang clothes in it."

Anna looked closer at the wardrobe, but there were no clothes inside it. With a shrug, she decided to turn her attention to the room they had stepped out into. It was obvious they were in someone's bedroom.

Alex—his composure regained—was already investigating the room. "Either the people who live here really like antiques or we have gone back in time."

Anna and Alex exchanged looks and then made their way to the door of the bedroom.

Mary was walking with a limp. It had been this way for more than half the day. Several times, she had stopped her fast pace to check inside her worn black boots for rocks. Each time she found her boots and her stockings damp with sweat but no sign of a rock or pebble in either shoe.

"A blister," she thought with dread. That was even worse than a rock. Rocks could be dispelled, blisters had to heal. And the only thing that healed blisters was time and medicine. Mary had neither, so she winced through the pain and quickened her pace.

With only her thoughts to keep her company, Mary allowed her mind to wander. *I wonder what the boys are up to,* she thought and smiled. It was well past noon, which meant they had already had lunch—*boiled eggs, probably,* she thought. No doubt they were enjoying their freedom. Mary smiled again. "Enjoy it while you can," she whispered. Once she found their father and brought him home, Morgan and Charlie would be back under his thumb.

Mary's smile dimmed. She couldn't block the image of the look on Morgan's face when she had left. Already three days had passed, but still she could see his sad, pleading eyes begging her not to go.

Her pace slowed. She had only been walking for three days and already she was beginning to doubt her bold plan. With no money in her pocket and just a small satchel of food, she had struck out down country roads alone in search of her overbearing husband.

Mary had thought that she would not be alone on her journey. She figured there would be other wives like her, who were trekking to nearby Crown Point in hopes of bringing their husbands home. She imagined meeting up with these women—they would laugh, trade stories, share each other's company, and perhaps some of the other women would even be generous enough to share their supplies. But it had been three long, cold, lonely days and she feared she was the only un-chaperoned woman walking the back roads of the countryside in search of the local militia.

Mary gulped back a wave of fear. The notice had said the militia was in Crown Point—but what the notice didn't say was how long the militia would be there. With the war as it was, the advantage of a small local militia was that they could move quickly and effectively to new locations on a moment's notice. It was possible that, by the time Mary got to Crown Point, the militia would be long gone.

From the comfort of her cabin, the plan to walk to this nearby town, while bold, seemed quite manageable. Now—after several cold, frightening nights spent in the woods alone—Mary was feeling that maybe Morgan had been right after all.

Doubt coated Mary's thoughts like a heavy fog. She had

only planned on being alone on the roads for maybe four or five nights, depending on her pace. Then, she figured, she would find her husband, talk him into coming home, and they would walk back together—safe in each other's company. But what if she couldn't find her husband? Worse yet—what if he had been wounded or killed?

Mary swayed from the fear her thoughts brought. Why? Why had she been so stubborn? Why hadn't she thought of any of this before? She slowed her limping pace to a staggering halt, whimpering as she felt standing weight on her right foot.

Blister, she thought with dread.

Mary looked up to the sky—it was between three and four o'clock, she figured. It would be completely dark within two to three hours.

Three days, she thought. If she decided to turn back now, it would take her three days to get back to her boys. She looked down the road in the direction from which she'd come. She could feel the warmth of her cabin and see Morgan and Charlie's smiling faces. Her own face softened.

Slowly she turned in the direction of the road ahead. With three days under her belt, she would reach Crown Point in one, maybe two more days. "Two days," she whispered. And if she couldn't find her husband it would be another lonely, frightening four or five day walk back. Her shoulders sagged. At this very moment, another week of walking sounded unbearable.

Mary looked back down the road towards her home and her sons. She already missed them terribly. Then she turned again towards the road ahead. *But I have already come this far,* she thought. Mary closed her eyes, trying to ignore the grumblings in her stomach. She rubbed her belly absentmindedly and opened her eyes.

Unable to make a decision and feeling her feet throbbing in her boots, she made her way off the path and found a large boulder by the side of the dirt road. She sat down heavily on the rock and eased out a long sigh.

"Well," she said out loud, "I might as well see about this blister." No matter what, she decided, she would have to tend to her aching foot. She clawed at her right boot, unlacing it clumsily. Then she slowly pulled it off. Her stockings were so damp with sweat and dirt that they clung to her foot like a second skin. Slowly she rolled them down, nervous to see what lay beneath. When she saw the large red welt-like blister on the ball of her foot, she nodded. "Blister," she said in resolution. "Great," she whispered.

It was foolish enough that she was traveling on her own, by foot, with no money and little food—but to have not brought any ointments or talc for her feet... Mary shook her head at herself. "What were you thinking?" she whispered.

She held onto her naked foot, wondering what she

could do. She had heard of women who knew how to work with plants and herbs, but Mary had never learned this craft. She knew about the basic herbs—chamomile, mint, sage, thyme... but she had no idea what herbs or plants would heal blisters or would alleviate her pain. She looked up to the sky. Time was slipping away from her—soon it would be dark and she would need to find a safe place to sleep.

Reluctantly, she grabbed at a random plant that stood behind the rock on which she was sitting. She peeled two small leaves off the plant and used them to cover her blister. Maybe the plants leaves would cushion the rubbing of the boot against her raw foot. Gingerly, she rolled her stocking back on and pushed her swollen foot back into her boot. But her blister felt worse now than it had before she had taken off her shoe. She bit her lip in pain.

Mary looked down the path. It would be a difficult and painful walk to Crown Point, but it would take less time than it would take her to return to her cabin and maybe she could find medicine in town for her blister. And if she were lucky, her husband would be there as well.

Mary stood and, with one final look back in the direction of her home, hobbled forward down the road towards Crown Point.

It was only minutes later that she heard the rush of running feet and screaming voices coming through the thickness of the woods to her left. She could tell it was men who were screaming, but she couldn't understand what they were screaming. Feeling scared and suddenly very exposed, she tried to hop quickly into the thickness of the woods to her right. But she couldn't hop fast enough. In her haste, she tripped and fell flat on her face.

The rapidness with which she was surrounded by yelling, bloodied soldiers with their muskets blaring, swords drawn, shocked her to the point of hysteria. She screamed, thrashing her arms and legs as the soldiers ran around her, over her, near her. But even with all her screaming, the soldiers seemed completely unaware of her. They were much too concerned for their own lives.

That's when Mary dared to look up, realizing immediately why she could not understand what the soldiers were yelling. They were—

"French!" Mary threw her hand over her mouth. The French—the very people her husband's militia was fighting—were swarming all around her. And even more, they weren't running towards a fight—they were running from a fight.

Mary tried to turn her face back in the direction the French had come from. Maybe it was her husband's militia that was after them. But it was no use trying to get a glimpse. Mary covered her head instead, trying to protect herself from the stampede of endless feet and legs running past her.

When there was a break, Mary pulled her body into a

ball, readying herself for a leap up and into the thickets that were so close. She closed her eyes. "On the count of three," she told herself. "One... two..." Right before she said 'three', she reached into the top of her dress and pulled out the small locket that hung on a modest chain around her neck. Inside was a miniature portrait of Morgan and Charlie. The year before, she had secretly saved money from their corn harvest to have the small portrait of her sons painted by a struggling artist. It was her most treasured possession. Gripping the locket in her right hand, she finished the count.

"And... three!" Mary jumped up in a burst of energy, surprising the already overwhelmed French soldiers. Ignoring their faces, she spread her arms wide and dove into the thickets. But as she was flying through the air, she felt something thick and hard stab her in the back. She screamed once before she hit the ground chest first—limp like a wounded bird.

I've been stabbed, she thought, her mouth filling with the taste of blood. She heard the retreating clamor of the French soldiers and in their place she heard the soft patter of different feet.

The militia, she thought hopefully, coughing and wheezing in pain. But Mary was only half right. She *had* been stabbed, not by a French sword, but by an Indian's arrow. And it wasn't the militia who were coming up the path in pursuit of the French soldiers. It was a small group of Mohican Indians—allies of the militia. When Mary had jumped up to reach the safety of the thicket, she had caught an arrow meant for one of the retreating French soldiers.

Mary heard footsteps coming through the thicket towards her. She tried to turn in the direction of the noise, but her body felt paralyzed.

"Who is it?" she gurgled, her mouth overwhelmed with blood.

The footsteps came closer.

"Who..." Mary stopped. She suddenly felt as if she was going to pass out.

Pahoma bent down and touched the back of the woman who had caught his arrow. She flinched under his hand. He knew by the direction and placement of the arrow that her wound was mortal. She had only moments left. He found her face with his eyes.

Mary saw the long black hair, deep penetrating eyes, and dark lined face of a Native American man staring down at her. If she could have controlled her body, she would have shot up and ran in fear. But as it was, she could barely control her own breathing.

He reached out, stroked her hand and spoke to her in a gentle tone. Mary could not understand what he was saying but something in his face told her of her fate. She was going to die—right here in these woods. Mary's eyes filled with tears.

"No!" she gurgled. *No!* she thought.

Pahoma continued stroking her hand and talking to her even though he knew she could not understand him. It didn't matter that she did not understand. He was responsible for her now. His arrow had brought them together.

"My boys!" Mary wailed, spitting blood from her mouth. She tried holding out the locket to Pahoma, but her hand was too weak. Pahoma noticed her gesture and opened her closed palm to reveal the necklace.

"My boys!" she wailed again.

Pahoma opened the locket and saw a small portrait of a young man with a young boy. *Her sons,* he thought. His face darkened. This mother would die and who would tell her sons? He pressed the necklace back into her hand and looked into her eyes.

"Where?" he asked in his language. "Where are they?"

Mary's body was shaking uncontrollably now. "My boys," she whispered. "I promised I would return."

"Where?" Pahoma repeated, urgently.

But Mary did not understand. "I'm sorry," she said to Pahoma, tears flooding her cheeks. She closed her hand on the locket. "I'm sorry, Morgan."

And then the life drained out of her.

Pahoma sat there with her for a long time, his heart heavy with guilt. And then, he took the locket from her hand and put it in his pocket. He would find her sons, he told himself. No matter what, he would find them.

Chapter Six

Now And Then

"I feel like I'm in a museum," Anna said in a hushed tone. "A kind of creepy museum," she added, a chill going up her spine.

Alex gave her a gentle shove. "Why are you whispering?" he asked, his own voice barely audible. "You're creeping me out."

When Anna and Alex had stepped out of the bedroom and into the main part of the house what they found was a darkened example of eighteenth century early America—cabin style.

"It's just weird," Anna said, trying to force herself to talk at a normal volume, "but it feels like a cemetery in here. It's all dark and like—" Anna stopped herself as another shiver tickled her back. "It just feels like something died in here." She wrapped her arms around herself.

"Yah," Alex agreed, "or at least left in a hurry." He was in the part of the cabin that was the kitchen. He touched a black iron pan sitting on a strange type of stove that looked to be a small fireplace. There was some kind of hardened pancake inside the pan. He poked the pancake. It wasn't just cold—it was rock hard.

Anna was in the living room area, studying the furnishings. "Why is everything so tiny? I mean, look at these chairs and the couch. They look like they were made for little kids." She shook her head in disbelief. "What time do you think we have gone back to?"

"1755," Alex said with certainty.

"Really?" Anna said, impressed. She leaned towards the couch. "You can tell the exact year from looking at the furniture?"

"Yah," Alex said, dryly. "You could if you were like some kind of freaky, obsessed antique specialist."

Anna looked up when she heard Alex's tone. Clearly he was not a freaky obsessed antique specialist.

"Or," Alex continued, "you could read this." He waved a piece of paper in the air.

Anna rushed over, all but forgetting the juicy comeback she had been crafting for Alex. "Lemme see," she said and she plucked the paper out of his hand.

"September 1, 1755. Lake George..." Anna's voice trailed off. "Lake George? But that's—"

"Keep Reading," Alex urged.

"Local militia in nearby Crown Point. Supplies needed." Anna stopped reading and looked up at Alex. "Lake George—that's right near our houses—now." Anna shook her head in confusion. "I mean not *now* now, because we're *here* now." Anna shook her head again.

"And here is near Lake George," Alex said. "Both now and then."

Anna covered her mouth.

"Or then and now," Alex added, "depending on your perspective."

Anna looked back down at the paper. "Where is Crown Point? I've never heard of it."

"It's a really small town north of where we live," Alex said, poking around the kitchen some more.

"How close it is to Lake George?" Anna asked stepping into the kitchen area with Alex.

Alex shrugged. "Dunno. Maybe like thirty miles or something. But that's not even the most interesting part." Alex turned and plucked the paper out of Anna's hand.

Anna made a face. "It's not interesting that we have gone back in time to the same area we live in present time?"

"No," Alex said, shaking his head. "That *is* interesting. But *more* interesting is the date on the paper."

But Anna had tuned him out. She was lost in her thoughts about where they had landed. "Why are we here?" Anna asked slowly, the hair on her arms standing up.

"Because we walked into a closet filled with orange yellow light in search of a kleptomaniac." Alex laughed at his own joke.

"A klepto what?" Anna said, confused.

"Someone who steals compulsively," he explained.

Anna gave him a blank stare.

"The kid, Anna. I was talking about the kid who showed up in your closet."

"Oh," she said, her mind wandering back to her question.

Alex rolled his eyes. "Jeez, it's not funny if you have to explain the joke."

"Yah, well it's not a joke if you have to explain it," Anna murmured, still deep in thought.

"You got me there," Alex said, smiling and shaking his head.

"Why are we here?" Anna asked again, more to herself than to Alex. "There is no sign of an assignment. No sign of anyone at all, actually—"

"Now, don't be so sure," Alex cautioned. "We haven't checked out the loft area."

Anna rolled her eyes. "Please, Alex," she said, "as small as this place is, and with as much noise as we've been making, our assignment would have to be dumb or deaf not to have heard us. And trust me, I saw the boy in my closet. He was neither of those things."

Alex's face grew serious as he put his mind to Anna's

question. "I see your point," he said slowly. "But what if our assignment was someone who could be seen when they wanted to be seen, and then not seen when they didn't want to be seen?" He raised an eyebrow.

"Your ghost theory," Anna said, nodding.

"It would explain why you think it feels like a cemetery in here." Alex shrugged. "Maybe he died in here," he added.

Anna felt the hairs on her arm stand up again and she scooted noticeably closer to Alex. "Yah," she said, her voice a bit shaky. "Well, first, I hate the word 'ghost' because it makes me feel spooked out. Just because someone dies doesn't mean they become something creepy or scary."

Alex thought immediately of Anna's father. It was his death that had brought Mama Do-Right into their lives. "Well, not 'ghost' then," he said. "Let's call it a spirit."

Anna continued standing close to Alex, her eyes darting around the small cabin. "It's an interesting theory, Alex," she admitted, her palms sweaty, "but why would we have a ghost—a spirit," she corrected herself, "as an assignment? What could we possibly do for a dead person? I mean we usually get assignments from..." Her voice trailed off and she turned and looked at Alex.

Alex's face split into a wide smile. "I think you just figured it out."

She smiled back. But then slowly her smile faded.

"What?" Alex said.

"If you were thinking what I was thinking—"

"Yah," Alex interrupted, impatient, "that this spirit is the one who requested your help and you haven't met the person he wants you to help yet - you know, you haven't met the assignment."

Anna shook her head slowly back and forth, unsatisfied. "But the boy in my closet didn't act like he was dead."

Alex raised an eyebrow. "How do the dead act?'

Anna huffed. "What I mean is he just seemed like a curious kid. He didn't say anything except—"

Alex cut her off. "Wait," he said, and reached into his back pocket for his small notebook.

Anna gave him a look. "You really have to check your notes for what he said? I only repeated it to you like twenty times."

Alex ignored her, flipped through his notes and then, with a smile, found what he was looking for. "He said—and I quote—'I want to fall awake'."

Anna gestured towards Alex's notebook. "Does that sound like something a spirit who wanted to tell me to go on assignment for them would say?"

Alex scratched his head. He didn't know all the details of how Anna got her assignments, but he knew enough to know that they were delivered by Mama Do-Right to Anna while she was dreaming, and that the assignments were usually given by someone who had crossed over to The New World who wanted to help someone they loved who was still alive on Earth. Alex flapped his notebook in the air and shrugged. "You've got a point," he said, nodding.

Unsettled, Anna began pacing in the small kitchen. "Mama Do-Right always gives the assignments."

"Yah, and you only get assignments when you're dreaming, which we are not doing right now." Alex squeezed his notebook into his back pocket and crossed his arms.

Anna stopped pacing. "But we *are* dreaming," she said.

Alex shook his head. "We're not. We can't be. We're not sleeping—or at least we weren't sleeping when we were in your bedroom."

Anna gave him a curious look. "Have you forgotten what Mama Do-Right said? And what about the axe? And the wardrobe that I opened with my imagination?"

"Mama Do-Right," Alex answered.

"What?" Anna said, annoyed.

"Mama Do-Right," he repeated. "Mama Do-Right used her magic to turn your closet into an orange ball of light, she put us back in time to 1755, and *she* made the axe appear and opened the wardrobe."

Anna rocked slowly back on her heels and crossed her arms. "Well, it sounds like Mama Do-Right has been busy." She made a face. "How unfortunate that she is not here to take credit for all her magical deeds."

Alex ignored Anna's tone. "She probably is here, knowing her." He turned and grabbed the pan that held the hardened pancake. "Maybe she is this pancake. Or... or..." he pointed to the small table they were both standing next to. "Maybe she is the kitchen table."

As a changeling, Mama Do-Right had the ability to change into any form she wanted, but Anna felt Alex was just being ridiculous. She cocked her head back. "Mama Do-Right is the kitchen table?" she said, mockingly.

Alex opened his mouth to reply but he was cut off by a loud sound from outside.

"What was that!" Anna yelled, jumping back.

"It sounded like a gunshot." Alex's face brightened. "A musket shot!" he said, excitedly.

"And that's a good thing?" Anna said giving Alex a worried glance.

"Remember when I told you there was something interesting about the date on that paper?"

Anna gave him a blank stare. "No," she finally said.

"Do you know what was happening in this area in 1755?" Alex began making his way towards the front of the cabin.

Anna trailed nervously behind him. "Let me guess—a battle?"

Alex turned to her, his eyebrows raised. "Not just a battle —a war—the French and Indian War." He looked like a kid on Christmas morning.

"And that was an important war?" Anna said, guessing.

Alex turned back around laughing. "Yes, Anna. It was a

very important war." His hand was on the handle of the front door now.

"Where are you going?" Anna said quickly.

"*We're* going out there," he said boldly.

"Do you really think that's safe?" Anna was pulling back on his arm.

"Why not?' said Alex, stealing a quick look at her. "We're dreaming, right?"

Anna let go of his arm. "Yah," she said, cursing her big mouth, "right."

Neither Anna nor Alex was prepared for what they saw once they opened the front door of the cabin. To be sure, they didn't really know what to expect, but they certainly didn't expect it to be...

"It's daylight!" Alex gushed, looking up to the perfectly blue sky about them.

Anna followed Alex's gaze, just as amazed as he was. "It's daylight," she whispered.

Almost at the same moment, Anna and Alex both looked back at the cabin. Lit up by the day's sun, now they could clearly see into the living room from the two windows that bordered the cabin's front door.

"But it was as dark as a cave in there just a second ago," Anna said, confused.

Alex was scribbling in his notebook. Anna took a step towards the front door of the cabin. As she reached her hand out towards the door handle, Alex screamed her name.

"Anna!"

Anna nearly jumped out of her own skin. She turned around prepared to scold Alex for scaring her to death, but when she saw his face and that he was pointing at something in back of the cabin, she followed his gaze until it landed on what had caused his outburst. Anna gasped.

"It can't be!"

"It is, Anna," Alex said, walking up behind her. "I would know that tree and that hill anywhere."

Anna covered her mouth in shock and then slowly turned to look around at the rest of the land surrounding the cabin.

What Alex had discovered sitting in back of the small modest cabin was the very same hill and tree that sat behind Anna and Alex's houses. They called it the Big Dirt Mound. It's where they had first spied on Mama Do-Right and where Alex had discovered (on the back side of the hill and under the exposed roots of the old tree) a hidden cave that he had turned into his secret laboratory. Now, it seemed, the Big Dirt Mound had a life that stretched back to 1755.

"Are you sure it's the same hill, the same tree?" Anna asked, turning back to Alex. "I mean nothing else looks familiar—nothing." Anna wanted Alex to be wrong because if he was right, it meant that not only had they traveled back to 1755 to an area near where they both lived in present time, but that they had traveled back in time and to the *exact* spot where their houses would be in the future. What could possibly be the meaning of that? Anna massaged her forehead.

"Anna," Alex said and gave her a look. "You know it's the same hill and the same tree. Look at it." He pointed towards the hill for effect. "It may be smaller than the tree we know, but that's definitely our tree and our hill. And we already know the cabin was near where we live in present time because of what the paper said. It all makes sense." Alex was getting very excited.

Anna bit her lip. "But why?" she whispered to herself. "Why?" she said to Alex.

"Why?" Alex repeated. "You mean why have we gone back in time over 250 years to the exact place where we live in present day?"

Anna just blinked a response and looked around again.

"That's a very good question," Alex said, answering himself. "I'm sure when we find our assignment it will all make sense."

"When?" Anna mumbled. "When," she repeated, "more like *if*." She shook her head and Alex was about to encourage her not to give up hope, when they were both rocked by more musket shots.

Instantly, Anna dropped to the ground. Alex spun around in the direction of the sound.

"Where did the shots come from?" Anna whispered, looking up from the ground. But Alex wasn't listening to her, but for the sounds of battle. "Alex?" Anna said, slowly standing up.

Alex motioned for her to stop moving. "Anna do you know anything about the French and Indian War?" He was still scanning the trees that surrounded the front of the house and the path that lead to a field far in the distance.

"The French and Indian War?" Anna hesitated. "Um—it was a war between the French and the Indians?"

"Not quite," he said and started walking towards the path leading to the fields. "The war was between the British and the colonists and the French and their Indian allies."

Anna started following Alex up the path. "But I thought the Indians were on our side—wasn't that the whole story of Thanksgiving?"

Alex stopped, turned back to Anna and gave her a curious stare. "Thanksgiving?" he finally said.

Anna shrugged weakly.

"Anna, nothing in history is a simple and perfect story like the story of Thanksgiving. The war was about land and money. Not all the Indian tribes fought beside the French. Some tribes—like the Mohicans—fought alongside the British and the colonists."

More musket shots were fired and now it was clear they were coming from somewhere past the field in the far distance. Alex crouched down and Anna copied his movement.

"If that paper we found in the cabin is recent and the date is accurate—then by my calculations, Anna, we could be very near to one of the most famous battles in the French and Indian War." Alex's face was flushed with excitement.

"But Alex," Anna said, trying to remain calm, "we aren't here on a history expedition. We're here on assignment. And—might I remind you—we haven't found our assignment yet."

"Exactly, Anna!" gushed Alex. "Remember what Mama Do-Right always says— there are no mistakes."

Alex made to stand up and Anna pulled him back down. "Alex, that has nothing to do with anything. We landed in the cabin for a reason. We should go back into the cabin."

Alex pulled his arm free from Anna. "There's nothing in that cabin, Anna. The action is out in those fields somewhere." He stood up quickly.

"Wait, no!" Anna said. "We wouldn't have landed in the cabin for nothing. There has to be something there." Anna was begging Alex with her eyes not to head out towards the fields. She didn't know why, but she had a nagging feeling that there was something in the cabin they hadn't found that was important to their assignment. Abandoning the cabin just didn't feel right.

Almost as if on cue, another round of musket shots was

fired. Alex was hopping in place. "Anna, it's the musket shots. We're supposed to follow them. C'mon." Alex ran a few paces down the path away from Anna. He looked like a wild horse ready to bolt.

Anna stood slowly, looked back once at the cabin, and then her shoulders slumped in defeat.

Alex cheered and took off down the path. "History, Anna," he called out without turning around. "We're going to see a part of history!"

As Anna ran to catch up with Alex, the same large brown eyes that had stared at them from the loft watched them now from behind the open front door of the cabin. But, there was a sadness in the brown eyes now—sadness and fear.

Chapter Seven

In the Fields

Charlie danced around Morgan as he made a slow trail between the fireplace stove and the kitchen table. It was the fifth day in a row Morgan had fixed corn pancakes for breakfast but to look at Charlie you would have thought they were having steaks. Charlie had been in the same carefree mood ever since their mother had left. *A week now,* Morgan thought, his eyebrows creasing together in concern. *She's fine,* he told himself. With any luck she would be back home in a few more days and then he could finally put all this useless worrying to rest.

"C'mon, Charlie," Morgan said and motioned for his brother to sit down at the table.

Charlie looked at the two plates, each with two corn pancakes, and he clapped his hands together. "Corn pancakes!" he shouted, genuinely excited.

Morgan laughed, in spite of his sour mood. There were many days he wished he were even half as happy as Charlie—how much easier life would be. Already Charlie was cramming bites of the thick, hard, tasteless pancakes into his mouth and licking his fingers in delight after each forkful. Morgan eyed his own plate of pancakes with a mixture of disgust and fatigue. Even his stomach gurgled its disapproval. But he didn't have the luxury of being picky. So with a slow hand, he lifted a forkful into his mouth and forced himself to chew and swallow.

"Today we work in the fields together—you and me." Charlie pointed a finger at Morgan and then himself.

Morgan nodded slowly. He was still trying to get down the first bite of his two pancakes.

"I am very strong," Charlie said, proudly. "I am a good helper."

Again Morgan nodded. It was the same conversation every morning. Most people would have been annoyed by now with Charlie's repetition, but Morgan found something comforting in the routine they had.

Each day, as the early morning light filtered through their small window, Morgan would wake and then gently rouse Charlie. The two would go together to the outhouse, and afterwards they would check on their cow and the chickens. If they were lucky, there would be eggs for their lunch. If there were no eggs, it meant they would have to eat corn pancakes for breakfast and then again for lunch. And if this were the case, Morgan would grimace and whisper "Thanks a lot" to the chickens, his face long. Charlie would echo Morgan's comments, usually laughing while he spoke. It never failed to crack Morgan up and pierce his bad spirits.

Before breakfast each morning, Morgan and Charlie rinsed their faces in the tall barrel of water that stood outside by the chicken coop. Sometimes Charlie would try to dunk Morgan's head in the barrel, which he found hilarious. But most of the time he just crowded in next to Morgan, happy as could be just to be preparing for their day together.

Once both boys were rinsed and dressed, Morgan would begin preparing breakfast while Charlie danced around. In between his jumping and spinning, Charlie asked questions about their mother—questions Morgan would have no way of truthfully answering. Questions like, "Where is Mother now? What is she doing at this very moment? What did she do last night?" To appease his brother, Morgan made up answers. And after a week of the same questions every day, Morgan had his answers memorized, and so their exchange sounded like a play being rehearsed. But no matter how many times they repeated their routine, Charlie's last question always affected Morgan. With each passing day he found it more and more difficult to hide his reaction from Charlie.

"Does Mother come home today?" Charlie asked while

Morgan forced the last bite of pancake into his mouth. Morgan knew this last question was coming as Charlie had already asked all the others. Morgan was relieved his mouth was full. It bought him a few precious seconds to manage his thoughts and his expression. He swallowed hard and then pushed his plate away in relief.

"If we're lucky, Charlie, then today is the day. If not, we're still lucky because it means we get to have more fun together—just the two of us." Morgan forced a smile.

"Just the two of us!" Charlie cheered.

Morgan's shoulders sagged—not that Charlie would notice. He was already clearing the table and whistling to himself. While Charlie's back was turned, Morgan released a long, hard sigh and shook his head in concern.

A week, he thought again. She'd been gone a week. As if that wasn't nerve-wracking enough, four days earlier while he and Charlie were working out in the fields, an old man had appeared high on the ridge—the other side of which lead to the main town. The old man seemed to be searching for something or someone. At first, both Charlie and Morgan had ignored him, but a moment later Morgan noticed that Charlie had dropped his sack and was jumping up and down. Morgan wiped his damp calloused hands down the sides of his frayed pants and looked up to see Charlie waving to the stranger on the ridge.

"He's saying hello, Morgan," Charlie said excitedly.

But one look and it was clear that the man wasn't waving

hello. He was motioning for them to come to him. His gestures seemed both dramatic and urgent.

"He's *really* happy, Morgan," Charlie said, continuing to wave.

"Yah, Charlie. It looks like that, doesn't it?" Morgan patted Charlie's back while trying to remain calm. Why would some old man climb the ridge to find them on the farm? Morgan's head swam with possibilities, none of which were good and one of which frightened him to his core.

"Mother," he whispered.

"Mother?" Charlie repeated. "That's not Mother. That looks like an old man." Charlie squinted for a better look.

"No, Charlie, you're right. That's not Mother, but maybe Mother sent him. Maybe he has news for us. Can you wait here?"

Charlie made a face. "Wait here?" he said, disappointed.

Morgan gave him a quick hug. "For just a moment. We're a team, right? You watch our crops and I will run to find out if the old man knows something."

Charlie still didn't seem convinced.

"C'mon, Charlie. You're strong and I can run fast. It's a good plan."

Charlie smiled slowly. "I am really strong," he said.

Morgan patted his back. "Yes, you are."

Morgan's conversation with the old man had been short. As he told it, he was there to warn them. There was a rumor that the French and their Indian allies were in the area, and that the British and the colonist militia were planning a battle. It was advised for local citizens to be careful, not to travel back roads, or wander too far from their homes.

When Morgan had asked if the old man had heard news of his mother, the old man looked confused. "Your mother is not here?" the he'd replied.

"No, she left three days ago for Crown Point in search of my father," Morgan explained.

The look that washed over the old man's face when Morgan told him this was something Morgan would never forget. It made his stomach turn to acid. The old man said nothing after that. Instead, he gave Morgan's slight shoulder a slow pat and then he looked across the field and waved to Charlie. Morgan turned to watch Charlie wave back. When he looked back at the old man, ready to thank him for the news, the old man was already making his way back down the ridge towards the town.

Ever since that day, Morgan had been plagued by the same dream. It always began the same way: He is working in the fields with Charlie—the sun is high in the sky. Charlie is in his usual good mood, happy to be next to his brother, and Morgan is filling sacks with corn. All of a sudden, Morgan hears musket shots. Frightened by the sound, Charlie drops to the ground. Morgan makes to drop down next to his brother when he hears his name called out. Instantly he recognizes the voice and stands back up.

"Mother," he cries out. "Mother!"

He hears his name again and he searches the field for her face.

"Mother!" he yells.

And then he hears more musket shots.

Morgan—forgetting about Charlie—runs out into the field, screaming for his mother. And then high on the ridge he finally sees her. She is smiling and waving madly just like Charlie would. And in that moment, he remembers his brother and runs back to get him. But he becomes confused in the field and he can't remember where Charlie is lying. He turns to find his mother on the ridge but she is gone. And that is when he wakes up from the dream. The feeling that he has lost his mother and his brother always stays with him for a while after he wakes. It's a devastating feeling.

"Morgan?"

Morgan pulled out of his thoughts to find Charlie smiling at him.

"Morgan?" Charlie repeated. "We have to go. The day is getting away from us."

Morgan smiled at his brother's use of their mother's favorite saying.

"You're right," Morgan said, finally, "the day is getting away from us."

"Here," Charlie said, innocently. "I saved you a pancake for lunch." He pointed to the large black skillet on the stove as he carefully wrapped his own pancake in a small, dirty handkerchief and slid it into his large back pocket.

Morgan stood up slowly from the table and made his way to the skillet. He eyed the pancake with disgust. After a second of deliberation, he rolled up his own dirty handkerchief and stuffed it—empty—into the front pocket of his pants. If he were lucky, the chickens would lay eggs today and he would make a big dinner.

"C'mon, Morgan." Charlie already had the front door open and was hopping from foot to foot.

Morgan took a deep breath. *Make the best of it,* he told himself, *if not for yourself, then at least for Charlie.*

"All right, Charlie," Morgan said, smiling. "The last one to the end of the path has to milk the cow tonight."

Charlie was out the door before Morgan had finished.

"Hey," Morgan yelled after him while racing to the front door, "that's cheating." And he darted down the path after his brother.

Anna caught up with Alex just as the path from the house ended. Stretching out before them was what looked to be miles of farm fields. The fields stopped right at the base of a high ridge. They could not see what was on the other side of that ridge. Anna pulled on one of the plants sticking up from the ground.

"Corn," Alex said, answering the question Anna was asking herself. "And by the looks of it, the crop is ready for harvesting."

Anna was used to Alex knowing just about everything, since he had been classified as a child genius almost as soon as he stopped wearing diapers. But there were some things he didn't know—things he couldn't see that Anna could sense.

Anna instinctively dropped to the ground and crouched on the balls of her feet. A split second later, musket shots rang out across the field. Alex dropped down next to Anna and, when he realized she had beaten him to the ground, he looked genuinely surprised. Anna opened her mouth to explain, but she was cut short by the sound of more shots being fired.

Anna gave Alex a worried stare and Alex brought his finger to his mouth, motioning for her to keep quiet. Anna nodded obediently. They peered up through the corn crop, trying to see if they could spot exactly where the shots were coming from. But with the height of the corn and their low position near the ground, it was next to impossible to see anything except—

"Stupid corn," Alex whispered and slapped a long stalk that stood near his arm. "I can't see anything," he added.

"Maybe that's not such a bad thing," Anna said, trying to ease Alex's frustration. But Alex had already made the decision that their position was pointless, and a split second later he was on his feet, racing through the corn, heading in the direction the shots had come from. Anna reached out to try and grab Alex back down, but she caught nothing but air.

"Alex, wait," she hissed.

"History!" he called back to her and continued running.

Anna silently cursed him and then stood and raced after him. It wasn't too long, though, before she started feeling disoriented in the long rows of tall corn and lost sight of Alex. Out of breath and frustrated, she stopped and kicked the base of some corn plants next to her.

This is ridiculous, she told herself. And it wasn't just the fact that Alex had run off without her that was ridiculous, or that she was lost in some huge corn field that was ridiculous. It was the entire assignment. She repeated the word 'assignment' in her head and kicked at the plants again. This was the furthest thing away from being an assignment that she'd ever been assigned to. For starters, she and Alex still hadn't found the person they were supposed to be helping. In fact, they hadn't found anyone. "And now I've lost Alex," Anna said to herself. "Ridiculous!" she shouted into the air.

More musket shots rang out. This time, however, they

sounded much louder than before. Which meant either Anna had moved closer to whomever or whatever was firing, or whoever or whatever was firing had moved closer to her.

Anna squatted close to the ground. *Where is Alex?* she thought, worriedly. She hated the feeling of being separated from him—especially when there was gunfire so close by. Of course, she reasoned, since they were dreaming it wasn't like they could get hurt, right? She considered her own question—unsure of the answer. Could they get shot, she wondered. Would they feel pain? Would they dream themselves dying but wake up from the experience as though waking up from a nightmare? Anna shuddered.

"I don't want to know," she said out loud.

"Know what?"

Anna jumped and screamed at the same time. Squatting next to her was Alex, his face flushed from running.

"Alex, you big jerk!" she yelled. "Where were you?" She swatted the side of his arm with her hand.

Alex put his hand over her mouth. "Shhhh..." he said, relaxing his hand slowly. "They're right over that ridge."

"Who's over that ridge?" Anna whispered.

"A small group of French soldiers," said Alex, his eyes sparking with excitement.

Anna moaned.

Alex's expression dulled. "What?"

"This is ridiculous," Anna whispered.

Alex opened his mouth to comment but Anna cut him off.

"What happens if one of us gets shot? Have you thought of that?"

Alex's expression shifted from one of annoyance to one of interest. "But you said we're dreaming," he countered.

"We are," Anna shot back. "But that doesn't mean we can't get shot or experience pain or death," she said, dramatically.

Alex sank deep in thought, rubbing his chin. "But we can't die," he said finally, "not if we're dreaming."

"Yah, well," Anna said, shrugging, "we could still *dream* we're dying and it could feel like we're dying."

Alex rolled his eyes. "Now *you're* being ridiculous."

"I'm... I'm being ridiculous!" Anna pointed dramatically at herself. "Alex, we're supposed to be on an assignment—not running after some French soldiers with *guns*."

Alex looked at her calmly. "So where is the assignment?"

"I don't know!" Anna hollered back.

"Shhhh!" said Alex.

"I don't know," Anna repeated in a loud whisper.

"Okay, well that's my point," Alex said, nodding. "Since we haven't found the assignment, we have to follow our instincts and mine say follow the gun shots. I mean you have to admit they are kind of hard to ignore."

"Those are *your* instincts," Anna said. "Mine want us

back at the cabin."

"The *empty* cabin," Alex corrected.

Anna gave him a look.

"Okay," Alex conceded, "come with me to the ridge to see the French soldiers and then after that we can go back to the cabin."

Anna studied Alex for a moment. "You promise?"

"Cross my heart." Alex made a crossing motion on his chest.

Anna's face relaxed. "Okay," she agreed, "deal. But don't run off without me and don't get too close. I don't want to risk my death or yours—even if it's only dream death."

Alex chuckled and shook his head. "Okay, okay," he said, smiling.

With their new agreement in place, Alex and Anna both stood up. And then Alex reached for Anna's hand. "C'mon," he said, "follow me."

With Alex in the lead and Anna gripping his hand, the two made it through the rest of the fields, which stopped at the base of the ridge. The musket shots were coming more frequently now and their sound was so loud, it was making Anna's ears ring. She covered one ear with her free hand and slowed her pace, pulling back on Alex.

Alex ignored her yanking, tightened his grip on her hand, and pushed forward at a faster pace. In this way, they made it to the top of the ridge in what felt like a short amount of time.

Once they arrived at the top, Alex released Anna's hand and motioned for her to take in the view on the other side of the ridge. Anna looked back the way they had come and was amazed that, not only could she see all the fields they had just run through, but she could also see the path that lead to the cabin and the cabin itself. Both looked very far away and very small.

"Anna," Alex said, impatiently. He tapped her shoulder. "You're looking the wrong way."

Anna turned towards Alex and followed his gaze down the back side of the ridge. What she saw made her stumble backwards.

"Oh my gosh..." Anna covered her mouth in horror. The scene below was a bloodied mass of soldiers, bodies, musket smoke, and what looked to be a small town on fire. It was obviously the remains of a battle. "Oh my gosh," she said again, her hand still covering her mouth.

Alex, in his excitement to show Anna an actual piece of history, had not taken into account how disturbing the scene below was.

"Sorry, Anna," he said quietly. He put a hand on her back.

Anna barely felt his gesture. All her focus was on the remains of the battle. "Who are they?" she said, finally.

Alex cleared his throat. "Well, with all the fire and the smoke it's hard to see clearly from up here, but it looks like maybe the French got the upper hand. But don't worry.

The French may have won down there, but the British end up winning the battle." He pulled Anna closer. "And the war," he added.

Anna's eyes filled with tears. "From up here, Alex, it doesn't look like anyone won anything down there." Unable to take in anymore, Anna turned away and took another look at the fields and the cabin in the far distance. That's when she noticed someone was waving at her. A boy. A very small—

"Alex!" she screamed. "It's the boy—the one from the closet!" Anna threw both arms in the air and waved them about madly.

"Anna," Alex warned.

"Alex," she said, her eyes locked on the boy below, "wave. Wave so he knows we see him."

"Anna," Alex said more urgently now.

"We see you!" Anna screamed. And then she waved for the boy to come to her. "Come up to the ridge," she hollered.

"Anna!" Alex screamed.

Finally Anna took her eyes off the boy and turned to Alex. "What is your problem?" she said, irritated.

Alex grabbed her head and pointed it towards the small burning village. Coming up out of the town heading in the direction of the ridge was a large group of soldiers. They were armed with swords and muskets and they were running.

"I was wrong, Anna. The French didn't win down there. The British did."

Anna, frightened, yanked her head out of Alex's hands. "What are you saying?"

"Those are French soldiers. It looks like they are retreating and they are headed our way."

"Oh no, Alex!" Anna turned back towards the boy down in the field, but he had disappeared. "The boy—he was just there. I was motioning him to come up to us. Where did he go? We have to warn him!" Anna was frantic.

Alex started running down the side of the ridge back towards the fields. "We can't see him because of the corn," he yelled over his shoulder.

"What will happen if the French see him?" Anna called out.

Alex stopped running and turned back towards Anna. One look at his face and Anna realized that it wasn't her and Alex who were in jeopardy of being killed—it was the boy.

"Anna!" Alex stretched his arm out to her. "C'mon, we don't have much time."

Anna closed her eyes and silently prayed. *Mama Do-Right, please help me help the boy.* And then she took off down the ridge.

Chapter 8

Lost

Morgan caught up with Charlie just as the path was fading and the fields were beginning. And it was no small accomplishment because, although Charlie had the mind of a small boy, he had the body and the legs of a tall, young man. When Charlie ran, he ran fast and far—covering long distances in a very short span of time.

"Gotcha," Morgan wheezed, struggling to catch his breath.

"I won! I won!" Charlie chanted, dancing a circle around Morgan who was bent over with his hands on his knees.

"Good job," Morgan said, straightening up. Above them the sun was out and already at full strength. They had let most of the morning get away from them. Morgan wagged his head in discouragement. Even with Charlie's help they were still struggling to manage the fields. One thing was certain, if his father did return, he would be angered at the site of the half harvested fields and he would blame Morgan.

"Come on, Charlie," Morgan said, sounding more sullen than he had meant to.

Charlie's happy expression faded. "Are you mad because I beat you to the fields? Because I could let you win tomorrow and then we would be even." Charlie smiled.

Morgan forced a smile. "No, Charlie. I am not mad at you. I am proud of you. You're very fast and very strong."

Charlie's expression brightened. "I am very fast and very strong," he repeated proudly.

"Yes," Morgan said, turning from Charlie to view the fields ahead. Morgan let out a tired sigh. "Come on, Charlie. There's work to be done and our day is slipping away. We'd better get to it."

Charlie looked at Morgan and then imitated his brother's serious expression. "Yes," he said, trying to sound like their father. "We'd better get to it." He pounded a fist into the open palm of his other hand for effect. Morgan caught the gesture—which took him by surprise—and he started to laugh. Charlie was quick to join him, his giggling like that of a child.

"I love you, Charlie," Morgan said, his laughter now under control. "You're the best." He hugged Charlie.

Charlie blushed and hugged his brother back. "We are

the best," he said and he held Morgan close.

After their hug and a few more pats on the back, Morgan and Charlie started into the fields, heading towards the spot where they had stopped the day before. Their task was simple. They needed to go up and down the rows of the field, collecting all the harvested ears of corn they could find. Each of them carried two large wool sacks that they would have to fill with corn. Once the sacks were full, they would each get two more large wool sacks to fill. It would go on like this until they had filled all two hundred sacks. Then they would carry the heavy sacks down to their cabin. Some of the sacks would go to the owner of their land, some would go to the town and be traded for supplies and food, some would be sold for money, and the rest they would keep to tend their animals and feed themselves.

When their father had left, harvesting season was right around the corner. Once the weather started to change and it grew colder, the race against time began. They would have to get all the corn harvested before the chill set in and the leaves began to turn. They were two weeks into harvesting season and Morgan figured they had another two, maybe three weeks left. But so far, Morgan had only made it through less than a quarter of the field and he had only managed to fill thirty-four sacks. Ten sacks sat near their cabin and the rest were sprinkled throughout the field. So that meant that, in the next three weeks, he and Charlie would have to finish the field and fill another 150 sacks, at least. Their task—although simple—felt daunting.

Morgan and Charlie quickly found the spot they had left the day before. Five large, full sacks were stacked neatly next to each other, and twenty or so empty sacks were piled on top of each other waiting to be filled. Robotically, Morgan bent down, grabbed two sacks for himself and handed two sacks to Charlie.

"We work side by side today, remember." Charlie stuffed one of the sacks into the back of his pants letting most of it drape down his legs. He held the other one loosely in his hands. When Morgan didn't reply, he added, "Morgan, you promised. Remember?"

But Morgan wasn't ignoring Charlie. With his head tilted up and his ear to the wind, he listened. "Do you hear something?" he asked his brother.

Charlie quickly forgot what he had been saying and listened along with Morgan. After a long, silent moment, he shook his head. "I don't hear nothing," he said and shrugged. "Why? What do you hear?"

Morgan shook his head. "I don't know. But there was—"

Morgan's voice was silenced by three loud musket shots. Instantly, both he and Charlie dropped to the ground.

"Did you hear that?" Charlie screamed. "Did you hear that!"

Morgan quickly covered Charlie's mouth, his hand shaking with adrenaline. "I heard it," he mouthed to Charlie. He motioned for Charlie to stay quiet and removed his hand from Charlie's mouth.

"Are we in trouble?" Charlie asked, forgetting to whisper.

Morgan shook his head. "No," he whispered. "We're fine. Everything is fine."

Charlie looked confused. "Then why are we hiding?" he asked innocently.

Morgan was trying to come up with a reasonable answer that Charlie would understand and accept, but his train of thought was cut off by another round of musket shots. Charlie's hands flew up to his ears.

"It's loud, Morgan," Charlie complained. "It's too loud."

"I know, Charlie." Morgan put a soft hand on Charlie's back. While he was comforting his older brother, he was struggling to remain calm. It wasn't just that musket shots were going off near their farm. It was that fact along with what the old man had told him, just days before, up on the ridge. Was it possible there was a battle going on nearby?

"The ridge," Morgan whispered. "Charlie?" Morgan turned towards Charlie. Both still lay flat against the ground under the shadow of tall corn plants. "Charlie," Morgan repeated and he pulled Charlie's hands down from his ears. Charlie turned towards Morgan, his face pinched in pain.

"Has it stopped?" Charlie said. "Has the noise stopped?"

"I... I don't know," Morgan answered, risking honesty. Charlie brought his hands up to his ears again and put his head down towards the ground. Morgan pulled Charlie's hands back down again. "It's going to be okay."

"It's going to be okay," Charlie echoed, his face still contorted in pain.

"Charlie, listen. I need your help and you're the only one who can do it."

Charlie's face relaxed, his eyes alert. "I can help you," he said, excited. "I can help you."

"Yes, Charlie. I need you to go back to the cabin and wait for me there. I am going to run up to the ridge and find out who is shooting. Okay?"

Charlie shook his head back and forth. "I go with you," he said. "I can run really fast and I am really strong," he added.

"You *are* strong, Charlie. You're the strongest. That's why I need you to go back to the cabin." Morgan paused, trying to think of a reason that Charlie would accept. "You need to protect our cabin and our animals. It's a big job and I can't do it."

Charlie looked suspicious. "For how long?" he said.

Morgan smiled, relieved that Charlie wasn't arguing with him. "Not long. Not long at all." He smiled again.

Charlie considered what Morgan had said and then he smiled as wide as his mouth would stretch. "On one condition," he said.

Morgan—starting to feel impatient—nodded quickly. "Anything, Charlie."

Charlie laughed and started clapping his hands together. "I get to light the candles. I get to light the candles!"

"Okay. Okay, Charlie," Morgan said, trying to calm Charlie down. "When it gets dark tonight, you can light the candles, but just this once. And you can't tell Mother."

Charlie silently squealed and clapped his hands together again. "I get to light the candles," he whispered.

It was a small thing to give in order to get Charlie to follow his direction. Even though he had sworn to his mother he would never allow Charlie to get close to either the fire pit or the candles—she was terrified he would get burned—how dangerous could it be to let him light a few candles? *And besides,* Morgan thought, *this is an emergency.*

"All right, Charlie. So you're going to go back to the cabin and wait for me. Do not come back to the fields. In fact, don't come out of the cabin. You just wait for me to come home, okay?"

Charlie nodded. "And then I get to light the candles."

"Yes. Yes, Charlie. Tonight when it gets dark, you can light the candles." Morgan started to stand up.

"And you'll be right back because it won't take long. It

won't take long at all."

"Yes, Charlie. That's right." Morgan was standing now and he reached down for Charlie's hand. Charlie—so excited—jumped up by himself.

"I go now, Morgan. I wait inside the cabin for you and I get to light the candles." He paused, looking suddenly confused. "But Morgan, what about the animals?"

"The animals?" Morgan said, forgetting his own lie to Charlie about why he needed him to return to the cabin.

"How am I supposed to watch over the animals if I can't leave the cabin?" Charlie seemed genuinely concerned.

"Oh right. The animals. Okay. Just... um... look at them when you get back to the cabin, and then go in the house right after. I'll be back quickly, okay?"

Charlie smiled. "Okay, Morgan. I'll do that."

Morgan patted his brother's shoulder and as Charlie turned to head back to the cabin, the sound of more musket shots rang through the air. Charlie screamed and Morgan ducked down. His palms damp with sweat, Morgan stood back up and gave Charlie a forceful push.

"Don't worry, Charlie. Everything's going to be okay. Just run to the cabin, check the animals, and then wait for me inside the house. *Don't* leave the cabin until I get there. Do you understand?"

"Yes, Morgan," Charlie said, nervously.

"Don't worry, Charlie. I'll be back before you know it."

"Before I know it," Charlie echoed.

Morgan gave Charlie another forceful push and then Charlie was on his way, racing through the corn fields as fast as a rabbit on the run. Morgan watched him for a moment, making sure he didn't stop or try to turn back. Once he could see that Charlie was safely heading back home, Morgan turned his attention towards the ridge.

Although the corn fields provided safety in the form of coverage (it was difficult to see much of anything or anyone between the tall corn plants), the ridge offered the only clear view of both the town below them and the area surrounding the farm. It was a bit dangerous to leave the safety of the fields and risk being seen by whomever was shooting, but only by going to the ridge would Morgan have a chance at discovering what was going on. This thought firmly in mind, Morgan ran as fast as his legs would carry him through the thick corn.

At first as he ran, his legs felt like rubber and his stomach was a ball of nerves. But as each moment passed without the sound of musket fire, his legs began to feel more solid and his stomach began to relax. There was probably a very simple explanation for the musket fire, he told himself. It didn't have to be a battle, he thought. Besides, if there were a battle, he and his brother would have been warned.

Immediately, Morgan remembered the old man on the ridge. *That was your warning,* he thought. But an old man, climbing up from the valley of the town three days prior to share a rumor—what kind of warning was that? *He was gossiping,* Morgan told himself. *Nothing more.*

Morgan came out of the fields and realized in an instant that he had been wrong. He had been terribly wrong. Running down from the ridge, heading straight for the field was a small swarm of soldiers. Morgan's first thought was whether the soldiers were French or British. A heartbeat later, his thought was, *Have I been spotted?* And his third thought disappeared with the sound of another musket shot. As Morgan fell to his knees and blood began to pool on the ground around him, his final thought was about Charlie. *I can't die because Charlie is waiting for me.*

Morgan slumped forward on the ground, his breathing shallow and his body numb. He closed his eyes for a moment and when he reopened them he saw no sign of the soldiers. *Odd,* he thought. They had just been coming down the ridge towards him. That's when Morgan saw her. Standing high on the top of the ridge, looking calm—almost happy—was his mother. He pulled his head up from the ground and realized that, although he had been hit in the chest with a bullet, he didn't feel any pain. *I must be in shock,* he told himself.

Morgan looked back up to his mother. She was smiling now and waving for him to join her.

"She's back," he said out loud, barely able to control the joy he felt at seeing her. Even better than the fact that she was back was the fact that she was alone. His father was nowhere in sight. Morgan took another quick scan of the ridge. The only person he could see was his mother.

His mother was waving more insistently now. "Come on," she seemed to be saying. "Come up here."

Morgan started up the hill that led to the ridge, but then he remembered his brother. "I have to go back for Charlie," he whispered. "Mother, wait!" Morgan screamed. "I have to go back for Charlie."

His mother continued to wave him up to her. "Come with me," she seemed to be saying.

"I can't leave Charlie," Morgan yelled to her. "He's down at the cabin. Just wait, Mother. We'll be right there. Hold on."

His mother did not stop waving him up to her, nor did she stop smiling. She looked as relaxed as a child in a field of flowers.

Morgan felt her happiness and smiled back at her. They were going to be all right. His mother was back. His father was gone, and Charlie was safe down at the cabin. Sure, he'd been hit by a bullet, but it couldn't have been too bad since he was able to stand and walk and he wasn't feeling any pain. His mother would tend to his wound and they would all be okay. For the first time in weeks, Morgan felt truly happy and relaxed. *Wait `till Charlie hears that Mother has returned,* he thought. *What a great day.*

"I'm going to get Charlie!" Morgan screamed to his mother. "We'll be right there."

Morgan turned away from his mother and her insistent

waving and began running back through the fields. He was amazed at how fast he was going even though he had been shot. Morgan looked down at his chest to inspect his injury and when he saw no evidence of a wound, no hole in his shirt—not even a speck of blood—he stopped dead in his tracks.

What's going on? he asked himself and a chill rolled up his spine. *I was shot. I remember being shot.* So where is your wound? his mind called out.

Morgan immediately turned around and began running back in the direction of the ridge. *Mother will explain,* he thought. *She will explain everything. And then she will go with me to get Charlie.* But when Morgan came out of the fields and looked up to the ridge, his mother was gone. Morgan dropped to the ground and began to cry. He wasn't sure what he was crying about, he just knew that he was suddenly very confused and very afraid.

And then it hit him—an explanation that made sense out of everything. *I'm in a dream,* he thought, *my dream—* the one with Mother and Charlie. Of course! Morgan dried his tears and almost laughed out loud. *All I have to do now,* he thought, *is wait to wake up*. Morgan smiled. And then he came up with a better idea. *Why wait to wake up,* he thought. *Why not just wake myself up?* Morgan was so proud of his idea that he gave himself a little pat on the back.

"Good thinking, Morgan," he said. And then he stood

up, turned back toward the direction of the cabin and started running home. *What a strange dream*, he thought while he ran. *I'll have to try and remember it when I wake up.*

"Where is he?" Anna said, out of breath. "Do you see him?'

Anna and Alex had made it down from the ridge and were just hitting the corn fields, but there was no sign of the boy anywhere.

"Maybe he's hiding," Alex said, pushing a large corn plant out of his face.

"But why would he hide? He visited me first, remember?"

Just then musket shots were fired from behind them. Both Anna and Alex dropped to the ground. Alex turned back to look up at the ridge. Running down from the ridge—guns and swords drawn—were about thirty French soldiers. They looked crazed with fear and fatigue. Speechless, Alex nudged Anna. But she wasn't watching the scene on the ridge because, less than ten feet from her, something far more intense was playing out.

Laying stomach down in a growing pool of blood was the boy from her closet. His eyes were open and his face was frozen in a look of shocked surprise. Anna's face held the same expression. And right before she was about to turn to tell Alex their assignment had just been killed, the boy and the blood completely disappeared.

Anna screamed. And then Alex screamed.

"They just disappeared!" Alex yelled.

"He just disappeared!" Anna yelled.

"Wait, what?" they both said at the same time. They looked at each other.

"Who?" they both said at the same time.

Alex put a hand up. "Wait. Did you just see what I saw?"

"The boy and the blood just vanished," Anna said nodding, her voice still loud.

Alex looked confused. "The boy? The blood? What? No—the soldiers. The French soldiers. They were coming down from the ridge and then they just—"

"Vanished," Anna said, completing his sentence. She was staring up at the ridge now, feeling just as confused as Alex looked.

"Where was the boy?" Alex was scanning the ground around them looking for evidence of blood or the boy.

Anna turned away from the ridge and found Alex's face. "There is something really weird going on here."

Alex rolled his eyes. "Well, thanks for stating the obvious, Anna. Tell me something I don't know."

Anna narrowed her eyes in annoyance. "Okay," she said. "The boy—our assignment—was lying right over there. He was shot and bleeding and it didn't look like he was going to make it. And then—" she snapped her fingers, "he just disappeared."

"Wow," said Alex slowly. And then his eyes lit up. "That's it!" he yelled.

"What?" Anna said. "What's it?"

"The boy, Anna." Alex stood up. "He's a ghost." Alex shook off what he said with a shake of his head. "I mean not a ghost—a spirit."

"The spirit thing again, huh?" Anna looked down for a moment and then back up to Alex. "Do you really think so?"

"He has to be."

Anna shook her head. "I don't know. I mean it explains the boy disappearing—maybe. But what about the soldiers? Why would they disappear? And how are we supposed to find a spirit—let alone help a spirit?"

Alex was going to tell Anna he didn't have all the answers, when he was cut off by the sound of someone running through the fields. Before Anna or Alex could react, they heard the sound of a young boy's voice.

"I can't leave Charlie. He's down at the cabin. Just wait, Mother. We'll be right there. Hold on."

Anna and Alex exchanged looks and then a moment later they were running through the fields headed back towards the cabin.

Chapter Nine

Pahoma

Pahoma had fallen behind the others, but he wasn't concerned. The others had seen his arrow hit the woman and then watched as he darted into the woods by the side of the road. They knew he was making sure she was all right—that he *had* to make sure she was all right. What they didn't know is that she had died while he watched her, helpless to do anything more than hold her hand.

Pahoma closed his eyes briefly. *Why,* he thought his eyes moist. Why had this happened—again?

Pahoma pulled his attention from his thoughts and focused instead on the terrain around him. He was looking for signs from the others telling him which way they had gone. It could be a broken branch, a rock overturned, a path of leaves flattened—signs which, to most, would be too subtle to notice. But to him—to each of them—the signs were very obvious.

A large branch hung down from a tall tree to his right. The top of the branch was broken and swinging like a limp arm. Pahoma dove behind the tree into the woods away from the main path. It looked as if they were going to try and race ahead of the French troops by taking a shortcut through the woods. Pahoma felt relieved. He hated the exposure of the main path.

Now that he was in the woods, the signs telling where the others were heading were easier to spot. Pahoma began a slow jog and quickly fell into an easy rhythm. It wasn't long before he found his mind wandering back to the woman.

What was she doing out on the road by herself? Pahoma had asked himself this question the moment she'd sprung up from the road, shocking everyone including him. His fingers had still been vibrating from the release of his arrow from his bow when he realized she was blocking his target. It had been an agonizing few seconds before the arrow punctured her back and pushed her forward into the woods.

"What was she doing by herself out on the road?" he said out loud, cursing under his breath. *Why,* he thought. *Why did this happen?* He'd killed a woman—a mother.

Pahoma's mouth filled with a foul taste. He started spitting—trying to clear the taste—but he knew it was pointless. He recognized the bitter flavor almost immediately. In fact, he knew it well. Ten years ago, he had been cursed with the same affliction. It had ravaged his senses for months after his wife and unborn child had been killed in a senseless battle. Nothing he ate and no amount of spitting could rid him of the horrific taste. In time, he came to know it as the taste of guilt and regret. Although it wasn't his arrow that had killed his wife and his unborn child, it was his fault there had been a battle where they could be killed.

A jab of pain stabbed his heart. Ten years had passed and yet it felt like yesterday that he had held his dying pregnant wife in his arms as the life drained from her. The bitter taste intensified and again he spit even though he knew it would do no good. He had killed a woman—a mother. And now her children's lives were in his hands.

Pahoma reached into the pocket of his breeches and pulled out the woman's locket. He opened it and looked again at the small portrait of her sons. The boy on the right—the younger one—he looked about the same age that his own child would have been if he'd lived. Pahoma closed the locket and put the necklace back in his pocket.

He was an excellent tracker—probably the best in his tribe. It was why his men were not worried that he had fallen behind and it was the reason they had found the small group of French soldiers and surprised them in an ambush. But even with all his skill, it was still going to be next to impossible to find the woman's sons. He didn't know her name. In fact he didn't know anything about her except that she'd been a mother, and she'd been poor and alone.

He had her locket and knew the road she'd been killed on—that was it. Was she traveling home along that small back road? Was she traveling away from home? The only town nearby was Crown Point. He'd just been there. It had been turned into an army fort and was overrun with soldiers and tribesman. It was no place for a woman. Of course, he reasoned, she could have had a husband and maybe her husband was a soldier. Pahoma turned that idea over in his mind but then quickly rejected it. No soldier would let his wife wander the back roads alone. *No,* he thought. She couldn't have been from Crown Point. So maybe her town lay in the opposite direction. In the direction he was now traveling.

Up ahead a large rock was stained with dark green smudges. Pahoma smiled, knowing handfuls of leaves had been used to make the mark. He turned left at the rock, his course now running parallel to the path where he had shot the woman. The French soldiers were being stupid and careless. They were choosing to stay on a path exposed and easily tracked. Pahoma quickened his pace. His tribesmen couldn't be too far ahead.

Pahoma found the locket in his pocket and turned it over in his hand again. Maybe all was not lost. If he could find the town she had lived in and show her locket around, maybe someone would recognize her sons.

Pahoma swallowed, the bad taste in his mouth subsiding. He would keep his promise. He would find the two boys, return the locket, and tell them about their mother. It wouldn't erase what had happened. It wouldn't bring her back, but it would ease his heart and—hopefully—the hearts of her sons.

His fellow tribesmen were in sight now. He could see them through the thick trees, not more than a hundred yards from him. They weren't trying to cut ahead of the French soldiers as he had thought. They were simply following them. *Smart*, thought Pahoma. They were letting the French soldiers think they had outrun Pahoma and his men. Then, quiet as foxes, they were following the French soldiers back to their post. And after that, a runner would be sent back to their British allies in the south, alerting them to their French enemy's position. A large battle was now in the making—that was for sure. The woman and her sons would have to wait.

"I light the candles," Charlie whispered. "I light the candles," he repeated. He sat in the dark cabin with his tall legs pulled up to his chest, rocking slowly back and forth on the small couch. He had been like this for hours.

When Morgan had not returned that morning from the fields, and when the afternoon had come and gone with still no sign of his brother, Charlie had begun to get very agitated. Several times he had even gone to the front door, prepared to disobey Morgan and return to the fields to find him. But he *really* wanted to light the candles, and he was afraid that if he broke his promise to Morgan and left the cabin, Morgan would break his promise to him and not let him light the candles. Charlie even wondered if maybe Morgan was testing him and was purposely waiting in the fields until dark to see if Charlie would follow his direction. And so Charlie allowed the afternoon to fade into early evening when he—with much excitement and joy—lit the first of many candles.

"See Morgan!" Charlie had yelled out the open front door. "I listen good. And I can light the candles!" he screamed. He had waited then, expecting Morgan to jump out and surprise him. And when Morgan did not appear, Charlie had begun to feel the first flutterings of fear. To calm himself, Charlie lit another candle. He placed both lit candles in the windows that bordered each side of the front door, one candle on each side. It was what his mother did when she was home and Morgan was in the fields past dark.

"You come back now!" Charlie had then yelled out into the darkness beyond the front door. And then he lit another candle. And another candle. And another candle. And he kept lighting candles until there were no more candles to light. In total, he had lit fifteen candles. It was a stock that normally would have lasted three months.

As the flames from the candles began to die and the cabin to darken, Charlie had begun to cry. He had been quiet about it at first, his tears falling silently. But with each passing moment spent alone in the dark cabin, Charlie had felt more and more frightened and alone and his silent crying had turned to loud sobbing.

But hours had passed since the last of the candles had burned down and now—spent and exhausted—Charlie sat in a ball on the couch, rocking and mumbling to himself.

"I light the candles," he repeated.

Charlie probably would have stayed like that for a long while if he hadn't heard a commotion coming from his parent's bedroom. Terrified, he sped up the stairs that lead to the loft and quickly hid in the shadows. When he heard the voices of two people—a girl and a boy—he nearly passed out from fright. Not only had they come from his parent's bedroom, which was strange enough, but they spoke with odd accents and were dressed very unusually—the girl was wearing pants!

He listened to them for a while, confused by their conversation. What was an assignment? Charlie was trying to muster the courage to come down from the loft and reveal himself, when both the girl and the boy started for the front door. Where were they going? Why were they going? It was pitch black outside. Charlie raced down the loft's stairs. No matter why they were going, he thought, feeling a glimmer of hope. If they were brave enough to venture out into the black night, maybe they wouldn't mind checking the fields for Morgan. That way, Charlie could still stay in the cabin as he had promised and Morgan could be found and sent home. Charlie smiled at his own brilliance. "I am smart," he whispered.

But when Charlie got to the bottom of the stairs, the boy and the girl were gone. Fearing he had lost his chance, Charlie screamed and ran to the front door. He swung the door open with such force, it nearly came away from its frame. And it was in that moment that Charlie realized that something very strange was going on. For outside, there was no sign of either the boy or the girl. It was as though they had disappeared.

Charlie stepped back into the cabin more confused and more upset than ever. He turned in circles for a while, madly rubbing the top of his head. And then he fell into the couch with tears in his eyes.

"Morgan where are you?" Charlie began rocking again, his tears tracing paths down his both cheeks.

Morgan stood directly in front of Charlie and watched in agony as his brother continued to rock and cry. He had never seen Charlie so upset. What an awful dream, he thought. He sat down next to Charlie on the couch and tried to comfort him.

"Charlie," he said. "Charlie, everything is okay. I'm right here. I'm right next to you."

Charlie stopped crying and tilted his head as if he was listening to something.

"Charlie," Morgan said. He reached out to his brother and tried to turn Charlie's face towards his so that he could see Charlie's eyes, but for some reason his hands couldn't seem to touch Charlie with any kind of force. It was as if his hands were no thicker than feathers.

"Charlie," Morgan said again. But Charlie had stopped listening and had returned to crying.

Morgan jumped up from the couch and screamed his brother's name. When Charlie still didn't respond, Morgan paced the floor in front of him and then stormed into the kitchen area and kicked the table. The table scooted violently across the wood flooring with a loud screech.

Charlie looked up. But Morgan didn't notice. He was so upset about being invisible to Charlie that he didn't see that Charlie was now staring at the table—his eyes wide with fear. Morgan put his head down and walked a straight line from the kitchen to the loft's stairs.

"I want to wake up," he said, fighting his own tears. "I want to wake up," he repeated, and he climbed the stairs and headed for his bed. Maybe, he thought, if he lay down on his bed and closed his eyes, this awful dream would go away. When he opened his eyes he would be awake.

But when Morgan lay down and closed his eyes, the horrible dream didn't disappear. He could still hear Charlie down below in the living room, crying. Morgan put his hands over his ears to try and block the sound.

"Wake up," Morgan told himself. "Please," he begged, "wake up." But still he could hear Charlie crying. Morgan jerked up from his bed. It was horrible hearing Charlie in so much pain. "Where is Mother?" Morgan asked himself. *Even in my dreams she's gone.*

At the thought of his mother, Morgan felt suddenly very homesick for her. *If I am dreaming, why can't I make my mother appear? Then she could comfort Charlie.* Morgan tried to imagine his mother's face in his mind, but he wasn't even able to visualize her hair. He stood up from his bed.

When he wasn't dreaming and he was missing his mother, which was often these last few days, he would sneak into her bedroom while Charlie was busy doing other things and he would climb into her wardrobe. His father had refused to have portraits done of anyone in the family including his mother. It was a senseless expense, he'd said. But he had allowed a purchase of an old wardrobe. And it was in this wardrobe that Morgan had found comfort. For although his mother had emptied it of the one dress she owned for her trek to find their father, it still held her smell—the fragrance that was uniquely her.

Morgan had discovered this when he was searching for an extra pair of pants for Charlie. Charlie had ripped the one pair he had and Morgan was hoping his father had forgotten one of his own pairs in his haste to leave. When Morgan had opened the wardrobe and found it empty, he was irritated. But then he caught the scent of something both musty and sweet. He poked his head in and inhaled. He swayed as the aroma that was his mother filled his lungs. It had surprised him when he felt tears stinging his eyes. He hadn't realized how much he missed her until he smelled her sweetness in that old wardrobe.

With a quick check to make sure Charlie was still occupied, Morgan had stepped into the wardrobe and closed the door almost shut. He had stayed like that for a while - breathing in his mother—feeling her all around him. He allowed himself a private moment to cry in her presence and show her his fear of being alone and apart from her. And when Charlie had called out for him, Morgan wiped his tears, bid his mother goodbye, and stepped out of the tiny wardrobe.

But it hadn't been goodbye. After that first time, Morgan had snuck in to visit her as often as he could. Aside from laughing with Charlie, it was the best part of his day.

Morgan couldn't see his mother's face in his dream, but he knew he had the next best thing. Maybe the wardrobe would help him find her in his mind and then he could make her appear in his dream and she would comfort Charlie.

"And then I can wake up," he whispered, "and be done with this bad dream."

Morgan made it down the stairs and through the main room, past Charlie who was now moaning and rocking on the couch. Morgan dug his fingernails into the palms of his hands and clenched his jaw. The only thing that would be worse than seeing Charlie this upset in his dream would be to see Charlie this upset in real life.

The door to his mother's bedroom was open and Morgan made a beeline for the wardrobe. He smiled in relief when he opened the wardrobe doors and smelled his mother's scent inside. "Mother," he whispered. He stepped into the wardrobe. "Mother, help me." Morgan closed his eyes. "Please help me wake up from this terrible dream."

And in that very instant, Morgan disappeared from the wardrobe—a fact he didn't realize until he opened his eyes and found himself in the shadowed closet of a young girl.

"Do you see him?" Anna was screaming back to Alex who trailed about a hundred feet behind her. She had run ahead of Alex, eager to get back to the cabin as quickly as possible. But in her haste, she had forgotten to keep a close eye out for the boy. One look at Alex told her he wasn't focused on finding the boy either. Alex had his head buried in his notebook and was scribbling madly.

"Alex!" Anna yelled. "The boy!" she whined.

Alex jumped, shoved the notebook back into his pocket, and sprinted to catch up to Anna.

"Jeez, relax, Anna," he said when he got up next to her. "The boy is headed to the cabin. That's where we're going to find him."

"Maybe," Anna said, impatiently. "And maybe he already got Charlie and he is on his way back to his mother."

Alex put a reassuring hand on Anna's shoulder. "Did you see *any* sign of 'Charlie' in the cabin?"

"No, but—"

Alex cut her off. "Did you see *any* sign of a woman or *anyone* in the fields or on the ridge?"

"No, but—"

Alex cut her off again. "Anna, your assignment is a spirit. Accept it already."

Anna gave him a look. "Just keep up, will you?" She didn't wait for a response. Instead she turned and continued running towards the cabin. When she arrived at the front door, Alex was right behind her, breathing hard.

"Are you trying to kill us?" Alex wheezed. "Why'd we run anyway? We should have flown. That would have been faster."

Anna had her hand on the door handle and, at the mention of flying, she mentally kicked herself for not thinking of it before.

"*Now* you say something," Anna said over her shoulder. And then she swung open the front door.

"We're baaack," Alex sang under his breath.

Anna kicked him.

It was a bright sunny day outside the cabin, but inside the cabin it was as dark as the night. Anna groped for Alex's hand.

"I can't see anything," she whispered.

Alex rubbed at his eyes. "Yah, that's because it was a bright sunny day just a moment ago and our eyes haven't adjusted."

As soon as the door opened, Charlie had stopped crying. It was as if his tears were drops from a leaky faucet that had suddenly been fixed. *Morgan,* he thought, and he jumped off the couch. *He's back. How foolish I was to think something was...* Charlie stopped. It wasn't Morgan standing inside the front door. It was the strange girl and boy from before. Charlie stood frozen in place, too scared to run.

It was Anna who saw Charlie first. He stood as tall as a tree in the middle of the room, dwarfing the small couch behind him. Anna reached out for Alex's arm when she realized that Charlie was staring at her. He looked terrified.

"Alex," she said out of the side of her mouth.

"Yah?" Alex whispered back loudly.

Charlie scooted nervously back against the couch and Alex, still unable to see clearly, turned in the direction of the noise. "Is he here?" he whispered.

Charlie looked at Anna, waiting to hear her answer.

Anna smiled nervously. "Yes," she said nodding to

Charlie. "And no," she added hesitantly.

Alex tilted his head in confusion. "Well is the assignment here or isn't it?"

Anna took a small step into the room. "Hi, Charlie. My name is Anna."

Alex rubbed once more at his eyes, and when he opened them he saw a large young man standing in the room with them, his huge hand covering his mouth as though he had just seen a mouse. "Charlie?" he said slowly.

Charlie nodded slowly. He had to admit that, although he was frightened and he had no idea how the girl knew his name, he was very relieved not to be alone any more.

"I am Charlie," he whispered. He patted his chest.

Anna and Alex stared at him, not really sure what to do or say. Charlie looked like he was almost an adult, but something in the way he was standing and in the way he talked reminded Anna of a small boy. Anna could tell he had been crying.

"Charlie, are you alright?" Anna asked, her expression soft with compassion.

Charlie nearly burst into tears. "No," he said, his voice cracking. "Morgan didn't come back. I lit the candles and he didn't come back." Fresh tears started falling down his cheeks. Anna raced to his side and grabbed one of his large hands.

"Don't worry, Charlie. We're here to help. Everything is going to be okay."

Alex had walked up and now stood on the other side of Charlie. He saw that Anna had one of Charlie's hands in her own and he started to reach for Charlie's free hand, but on second thought he decided to pat Charlie's back instead.

Charlie looked at Alex and patted his chest. "I am Charlie," he whispered.

Alex smiled. "My name is Alex."

Charlie smiled and nodded. "Alex and Anna." He turned to Anna. "Can you help me find Morgan?" he said innocently.

Anna smiled. "Yes, Charlie. That's exactly what we're here to do."

Neither Anna nor Alex heard the bedroom door open. So neither of them noticed when Morgan stepped into the room. And when he spoke, they both jumped.

"What are *you* doing here?"

Chapter Ten

Nightmare

Where Pahoma was getting his energy to stand he did not know. Every bone and every muscle in his body ached. They had been severely outnumbered in the battle, and at one point it had looked as if this would be their downfall. But the British were clever and the colonists brave. And with the help of his people, they'd been able to drive the French back and win. Of course, this was no cause for celebration. There would be many more battles fought before this war was settled. But a victory was a victory and all around him, tired, worn-out men just like him smiled with pride. Pahoma nodded to them as they passed. There was no pride for him in killing. To him war was something necessary but not something enjoyed.

The tedious part of the battle was now underway—the cleanup. Men were counted. The wounded were tended to and the dead buried or burned. Enemy soldiers wounded or captured were rounded up and guarded. For Pahoma and his fellow tribesmen there was nothing to do but watch. They had offered their assistance as scouts and warriors and that was all. Besides, they had their own men to tend to.

Pahoma walked slowly down the street, his face stoic, his body rigid with aches. He had been lucky. His wounds were minor. Others from his tribe had not been as fortunate. He had found an abandoned stable at the far end of town where his wounded men could rest and be cared for. Now he walked through the burning remains of the town looking for any of his own he had not already found.

It was a pity about the town. The French had burned most of it down before the British were able to regain their control. Most of the townspeople had fled before the fighting had begun, but there were a few stubborn families who had refused to abandon their homes. Pahoma saw some them walking through the wreckage looking sorrowful and lost. They stayed to save their homes and in the end they stood by—helpless—as their homes and all they owned were turned to ash. Pahoma would never understand why the white men were so attached to their things that they would risk their own death or the death of their families.

Pahoma was only halfway through the town when one of his own called out his name and ran to catch up with him. Pahoma recognized him immediately as his tribe's translator – the one who could speak and understand the white man's language. Trailing behind his man was a British soldier. Pahoma exhaled slowly. *What now?* he thought.

"It's the boy from my closet," Anna whispered to Alex. "You're the boy from my closet," she said to Morgan, stunned to finally be face to face with him.

"What are you doing here?" Morgan repeated. He couldn't figure it out. Just a moment ago he had been in her closet reading her book about falling awake. And then she had opened the closet door, surprising him, and in an instant he found himself back in his mother's wardrobe. And now she was standing in the main room of his cabin. This was a very peculiar dream.

Charlie was totally confused. "Who are you talking to, Anna?" Charlie said. He looked at the door to his parent's bedroom. It was clear to him that Anna and Alex were startled by something, but there was definitely no boy standing there. "Do you see a mouse?" he asked.

Anna looked at Charlie and then back at Morgan and then at Alex. Alex shrugged.

"He can't see me," Morgan explained. "I know it's my dream and I should be able to make him see me, but I've tried and I just can't get him to see me."

Anna was trying to make sense of the situation when

she heard Morgan say the word *dream*.

"Wait, what?" she said to Morgan.

"Who are you talking to?" Charlie asked again. It was bothering him that Anna was talking to the dark. Was she crazy or was he really not able to see something that was there? "There's no one there, right?" He looked at Anna and then Alex and then back at Anna.

"Wait," Anna said to Morgan and then she turned to Charlie. It was obvious that the boy standing near the bedroom door was the boy she had seen in her closet. And it was also obvious that Charlie couldn't see the boy. What wasn't obvious was why or how the boy had made it into her closet in the first place and why Charlie couldn't see him. And even more, she wasn't sure who the boy was. Was he Morgan—the one Charlie was fretting over finding? Was the boy the one she and Alex had heard talking in the field? She had a lot to find out, but she didn't want to upset Charlie. She and Alex had just managed to calm him. Anna had an idea. "Charlie, have you ever had an imaginary friend?"

Charlie wrinkled his eyebrows. "A what?"

"You know—a friend that no one else could see but you?"

Charlie thought for a long moment and then he smiled. "Yes!" he said, excitedly. "When I was really little, before Morgan was born, I had a friend just like that. Mother and Father never saw him because he was really shy and only played with me when they weren't looking. He was fun."

Anna gave a relieved sigh. "Okay. So Alex and I have an imaginary friend and he wants to talk to me. Is that okay?"

Charlie frowned. "Why can't I see him?"

"Well... he's really shy, too," she said, praying he would accept her explanation without asking more questions.

Charlie was still frowning, disappointed that he was not being included, but he understood about being shy. When he was around other kids, he was mostly shy, too. "Okay, but when he is done being shy, can I see him then?"

Anna glanced at Alex hoping for some support and direction. But Alex didn't catch her looking at him. He was so lost in what was happening, he forgot he was part of what was happening.

"Alex," Anna said, annoyed. "Charlie wants to know if he could see our imaginary friend later when our friend is done being shy. What do you think?" She was desperate for his help.

"I... well... I mean..." Alex stammered. He glanced at Morgan who was still staring holes into Anna. "Um... yah... if our friend isn't shy later. Um, sure?"

Alex had ended his stammering with a question in his voice. If Charlie hadn't been staring directly at Anna, she would have slapped her own forehead in frustration. *Nice job, Alex,* she thought, mentally rolling her eyes. But it had worked. Charlie's frown had turned into a smile and he stared expectantly at the space next to his parent's bedroom door. He was waiting for Anna and Alex's friend to not be shy so he could see him too.

With Charlie taken care of, Anna was ready to question the boy and finally get some answers about what was going on. But when she turned to find Morgan, he was gone.

"Alex!" she screamed.

Both Alex and Charlie jumped. Alex looked up from his notebook. After he had spoken to Charlie, he had grabbed for his notes. He'd wanted to jot down a few thoughts he had about what was happening. But once again, in his earnest effort to keep an accurate record of what was going on, he'd missed something important.

"He's gone!" Alex said, realizing immediately why Anna was freaking out. "But he was just there!"

"Did I scare him away?" Charlie worried. "I am kind of tall."

Anna was beside herself with frustration. "I give up!" she yelled to the ceiling. "This is ridiculous," she said to herself.

"I'm telling you," Alex said, reading back through his notes, "everything points to the fact that this kid is a—"

"Alex," Anna warned, her eyes darting towards Charlie. "Don't."

Alex took a step back so he was standing slightly behind Charlie and he mouthed the word *spirit.*

"A lot of kids are afraid of me," Charlie said sadly. "I probably scared him."

Anna stopped fretting for a moment and patted Charlie's big hand. "No, Charlie. It wasn't you. It was... It was..."

Charlie waited for Anna to finish, his eyes as wide and innocent as a small child's.

Anna sighed long and hard and then looked down. "I'm not sure why he disappeared." She looked back up and took a deep breath. "But don't worry. I'm sure he will be back."

The British soldier was a small, frail looking man with thinning blond hair and pale skin. He wore tiny spectacles and Pahoma marveled at how clean his uniform was. Pahoma ventured that, not only had he not participated in the battle they'd just won, but the soldier had never been in battle.

Pahoma waited patiently while the soldier spoke to his man. He didn't understand a word of English but it was clear from how the soldier was speaking that he was agitated about something. *What was this about*? Pahoma asked himself again.

Finally the soldier took a breath and Pahoma's man was able to turn from him and explain what had been said.

"About thirty French soldiers were seen leaving the town. Probably over that ridge." Pahoma's man motioned to a place behind Pahoma's back. Pahoma did not turn around.

"What does that have to do with us? Or with anything? How much harm can come from thirty French soldiers?" Every part of Pahoma's body begged him to lie down and rest. They had been tracking and fighting for days before the battle they'd just fought in began. Hadn't they done enough? At the very least they had earned a day's rest.

"The French soldiers who were seen retreating were carrying important papers. The papers give detailed information about the British army and their battle strategies."

Pahoma rubbed his tired eyes. "How does he know that?" He motioned towards the soldier. "How can they know that?"

Pahoma's man looked at the soldier and said something Pahoma did not understand. The soldier responded almost before Pahoma's man had finished talking. He seemed very nervous.

"Well?" Pahoma asked, his patience thin.

"There was a traitor among the French soldiers. A British traitor." He recognized the look on Pahoma's face. Pahoma was not happy. Pahoma's man looked down.

"We track your enemy, lead you to your enemy, and help you kill your enemy and you can't manage to take care of your own people?" Pahoma yelled at the soldier. The soldier shrunk back in fear. Pahoma stood over six feet tall and his face was dark and lined from age and sun exposure. His black hair hung long down his back and matched the color of his eyes, which were, at this very moment, filled with anger. The soldier had no idea what Pahoma was saying but it was clear, he was not happy with the news.

Pahoma's man was smart enough to keep quiet. He knew that Pahoma would end up agreeing to help the British recover the runaway French soldiers, but he also knew that it would take a few moments for Pahoma to warm up to the idea.

"How many do we have who are not wounded?" Pahoma finally asked. He was now turned towards the ridge. The soldier took this as a positive sign and straightened up. He figured Pahoma was structuring a plan, but that couldn't have been further from the truth. Pahoma wasn't staring up at the ridge thinking about the escaped French soldiers. He was staring up at the ridge thinking about the woman he had shot and her two sons. He hadn't forgotten his promise.

"How am I going to find your sons?" he whispered to himself.

"What?" said Pahoma's man.

Pahoma shook his head and turned back to the soldier who looked a bit less nervous now. "I will track for two days. If we find them in that time, then we find them. If we don't find them, then we don't. That is all I will offer."

Pahoma's man quickly translated what Pahoma had said and the soldier, sighed in relief. "That's fine. That's more than fine. It's great. Thank you," he said to Pahoma's man. "Thank you," he said—a bit louder—to Pahoma.

Pahoma ignored him and turned back the way he had been walking before he'd been interrupted. "I will need six," Pahoma said over his shoulder. "Have them meet me back here."

Pahoma's man nodded and started toward the stables to gather the six men Pahoma had requested.

"Wait," said the soldier, confused. "Why is he walking away? I thought he said he would help."

"He did say he would help," said Pahoma's man, impatiently.

"Then why is he walking away? The French fled up that ridge." The soldier fidgeted nervously.

Pahoma's man shook his head. "It is not for me to question. He will find your French for you." And with that Pahoma's man ran off towards the stables.

Morgan stood in the middle of the fields confused. Afraid, really. What had just happened? A moment earlier he had been in the darkened cabin with Charlie, the girl from the closet, and her friend. And now he was outside in his fields in the middle of the day with the bright sun on his face. He sat down slowly, his eyes darting around nervously.

"What is going on?" he said. "Why am I having this dream and why can't I wake up?" Morgan put his head in his hands.

He had to admit that the entire dream hadn't been awful—just the parts with his mother and Charlie. The part of his dream where he was in the girl's closet and then her room was actually exciting. There were so many interesting things there. The most interesting thing being the book she had—the Falling Awake book. It talked about how you could control your dreams and travel wherever you wanted.

What good is that doing me, he thought, suddenly feeling very depressed. *I can't even control where I am.* Morgan ran his hand along the dirt in front of him. Of all the places in the world he could be, the last place he wanted to be was in these fields. And yet here he was. *A nightmare,* he thought, shaking his head sadly.

And then he could have sworn he heard someone say his name. Morgan sat up, his ears alert. He thought he heard it again. Morgan stood now, looking around.

"Who's calling me? Who's there?"

"Morgan." The voice was louder now. And it seemed to be coming from somewhere in the corn fields. Was it a woman's voice?

"Who are you?" Morgan called out. He began walking in the direction he thought the voice had come from.

"Where are you?"

As Morgan walked through the fields, the voice continued calling his name. It went on like this for what felt like a long time until Morgan realized he was coming to the edge of the cornfields. Up ahead was the ridge. That's when he saw her. Standing on top of the ridge, just as before, was his mother. She smiled and waved at him to come up to her. She looked more happy and peaceful than he had ever seen her look.

"Mother?" he said, unsure. "Is this is a dream?"

He heard his name again and she continued to wave to him. Morgan thought of Charlie and how happy he would be to see their mother, even if it was just a dream. He looked back into the cornfields in the direction of the cabin. *How would I get Charlie to come back here with me? He can't see me.*

Morgan looked back at his mother, afraid she would disappear just as she had before. *The girl could help me,* he thought. *The girl and her friend can see me.* Morgan turned again in the direction of the cabin. He even took a step back into the fields. *But wait,* he thought. *What if the girl and her friend are gone? And what if Mother disappears again? No,* he thought. *I can't risk it. I have to go to Mother. I will tell her to come back with me to the cabin and then Charlie can see her.* Maybe then he would finally wake up from this very strange dream.

Morgan turned and waved at his mother, who was still

smiling. "I'm coming, Mother!" he yelled. "Just wait, I'm coming!"

Morgan ran out of the fields and headed up the hill that led to the ridge. He was thrilled that he would get a chance to hug her. Even if it were just a dream, it would still feel real. But Morgan only made it halfway up the hill before he stopped dead in his tracks. Coming down from the ridge was a small group of the fiercest looking Indians he had ever seen.

"Mother!" he cried out. But his mother was nowhere to be seen. "No!" he yelled. And then he realized that one of the Indians—the tallest and most intense of them—was staring right at him. Morgan stumbled back in fear. But worse than that, it looked like the Indians had changed their course and were now coming to get him. Morgan let out a loud scream and ran down the hill towards the fields as fast as his legs would carry him. He had to warn Charlie. Dream or no dream, those Indians meant business.

Please, he thought. *Please let the girl still be there in the cabin.* It would be his only hope of warning Charlie.

Pahoma trudged up the hill towards the ridge, away from the burning town, with six of his men trailing behind him. They were all weary from battle and tired of tracking the French, but they had pledged their allegiance to the British and the colonists and their word meant something.

And so they followed Pahoma up the hill, fulfilling their duty.

It was late afternoon and early fall so the weather was fair. Even so, Pahoma and his men began to sweat. *I hope the French fled to a place near a river,* thought Pahoma. He was ready for a cold swim and a long drink.

Once they reached the top of the ridge, they could see the beginnings of a modest corn farm, a small cabin in the distance, and then forest. Pahoma released a tired sigh, not caring that the others would hear it. It was pointless to try and disguise his fatigue. He would have to be something other than human not to be exhausted by now.

He and his men began walking down the other side of the ridge toward the cornfields, their eyes alert to any signs that the French had passed this way. Pahoma was the first to see the body.

At the edge of the corn fields, almost hidden by the large plants, lay a small figure. Something in the way the body was placed made Pahoma think whoever it was had been shot. But there was something else about the body that struck Pahoma. It was small. Very small. In fact, it was too small to be that of a man. Was it a woman? Pahoma saw pants. *No,* he thought. The white women wore dresses.

"It's a child," Pahoma said to the others. And they all changed direction to investigate.

Pahoma reached the body first. It was a boy—a boy of no more than ten, he thought. And then it suddenly occurred to Pahoma to check the boy's face. When he did, he almost fell back in shock. Although he had never met him, Pahoma would have known that face anywhere. Pahoma reached into his pocket and pulled out the woman's locket, opening it to reveal the portrait inside. He covered his mouth, still suffering disbelief. It was one of the woman's sons—her younger. Pahoma felt a deep sadness he could not completely understand.

Standing around him, his men were quiet, but Pahoma knew they were wondering what was going on. They had all seen many bodies during the course of their battles—some were women and some were children. Although it was sad, it wasn't something they would have reacted to so intensely. It was not as if Pahoma had killed this child.

I'm so sorry, Pahoma thought and he touched the boy's face. He had killed this boy's mother and then she hadn't been there to defend her child. He now had two deaths on his conscience. It was a dark moment for him.

"Pahoma?" said one of the men. "Pahoma, we will lose their trail if we stay here much longer. The boy is dead. Let's leave him in peace."

Pahoma hung his head, feeling the bitter taste come back into his mouth. He wiped remorsefully at his lips. He stared back down at the locket and the portrait inside and then it hit him. Wait, he thought. *The boy. The mother. This is their farm. The other son—he must be nearby. Maybe in the cabin—if he was lucky enough to avoid the French.*

"Pahoma?" said one of his men. "We need to go."

Pahoma stood so quickly it startled the other men. "No," he said. "You all go on. The trail is easy to pick up right now. They can't be more than a few hours ahead. I have unfinished business here." He turned and faced their stares. "Don't worry. I will catch up with you."

The men stared at the boy's body and then at Pahoma, confused. But they knew Pahoma well enough to know that he would offer no more explanation—even if they pushed for it. So with nods of acceptance, they turned and made their way along the edge of the cornfields, aiming for the forest beyond. They knew Pahoma would honor his word and meet up with them soon.

Once his men were on their way, Pahoma knelt back down and placed his hand on the boy's body. "If your brother is alive," he whispered, "I will make my amends to him for you and your mother. Whatever he needs, I will give him."

And then Pahoma stood up and began making his way through the fields towards the cabin.

Chapter Eleven

Change

"They're coming! I saw them. They're coming!" Morgan stood just inside the front door of the cabin, his eyes wild with fear. Unlike before when he had disappeared from the cabin and reappeared instantly into the fields, this time he'd had to run all the way back from the fields in order to return to the cabin. What struck him right away when he entered his house was that it was daytime. Not like before when it was the dark of night. The other thing that struck him was that the girl, the boy, and Charlie were crowded together on the couch and the girl and the boy were staring at him as though he were a ghost. Neither of them reacted to what he had just said.

"I'm telling you," Morgan yelled, "they're on their way!

We have to get out of here!"

Anna and Alex stared dumbly at Morgan. They were still suffering from the shock of his return, among other things. For as soon as Morgan had walked into the cabin, it had become suddenly daylight and Charlie, who had been wedged between them on the couch, was now in the kitchen rummaging for something and whistling.

"He's back," Alex whispered, stating the obvious.

"Yah," Anna said slowly, "I got that part. But what's up with Charlie and why is it suddenly daylight?"

"Why aren't you listening to me!" Morgan screamed at them. "And why won't this awful dream end?" he cried to himself. Morgan went to one of the front windows and peered out. He couldn't see anyone yet, but it was just a matter of time. Those Indians were intense and they had definitely seen him, especially the really tall, scary looking one. Morgan turned to Anna. "You have to help me get Charlie out of here," he said, desperately.

Before Morgan had returned, Anna, Alex, and Charlie had been sitting crammed together on the small couch. It had definitely not been the most comfortable seating arrangement since the couch was small and Charlie was big, but there weren't a lot of other seating options in the cabin where all three of them could stay together. At least, that is what Anna had told herself. In truth, none of them had wanted to sit by themselves. The dark cabin had been a bit creepy and it hadn't helped matters when Morgan had vanished into thin air. Anna wasn't sure how long Morgan had been gone for, but it had been long enough for her and Alex to learn quite a bit from Charlie. For starters, the boy from Anna's closet was Charlie's brother, Morgan.

"I get to light the candles when Morgan gets back," Charlie sang to himself. His back was still facing the main room as he continued digging for more candles. Already, he had gathered ten.

Anna looked worried. "I don't understand what's happening," she said to Alex. Charlie's acting like we're not even here."

Alex nodded slowly, his eyes still on Morgan. "I know, but I think we have more pressing issues than what's going on with Charlie." He motioned towards Morgan.

Anna was feeling confused and tired and overwhelmed. Nothing made sense to her. She still wasn't even sure if Morgan was her assignment or if Charlie was her assignment. Anna rubbed her forehead.

What they had learned from Charlie was that he and Morgan had been alone in the cabin for a while because their mother had journeyed to find their father. Charlie told them there had been some loud noises as he and Morgan worked in the cornfield and that Morgan had told him to go back and watch the cabin and animals until he returned from seeing where the noises were coming from. He had also told Charlie he would be back quickly. But he hadn't come back all day and then, sometime in the night,

Anna and Alex had shown up.

But of course all this was Charlie's version of the story, because Morgan *had* returned—twice. But that's where it became confusing because, for some reason, Charlie couldn't see Morgan, Morgan kept saying he was in a dream, and Anna had seen Morgan's body in pool of blood out in the fields. Was Morgan dead and now a spirit walking around—unaware he was dead? Or was Morgan dreaming and Anna and Alex were in his dream? Or were they in Charlie's dream? Anna rubbed her forehead again. She didn't really know what was going on. What she did know was that Morgan was very upset about something.

"Who is coming?" Anna finally said to Morgan.

At the sound of Anna's voice, Charlie jumped and twisted around—startled and terrified. He jabbed his hand, which was crammed full of candles, towards Anna and Alex and screamed. "Who are you? And what are you doing in here—this is my house! This is my house with Morgan and he is going to come back and be very mad that you are here." Charlie—all six feet of him—was shaking.

Anna, Alex, and Morgan all stared back at Charlie in disbelief. "Charlie," Anna said slowly. "Don't you remember? We met last night. I'm Anna and this is Alex—we're here to help you find Morgan." Anna stood up slowly from the couch. Charlie jabbed the candles in the air towards her and scooted back violently.

"Stay away from me!" he screamed. "I was with Morgan

last night and he is in the fields now and he is going to come back soon and he will be very angry with you. I am protecting the cabin and our animals. You can't be here." Charlie tried to stand tall and show that he was brave, but his legs wobbled uselessly underneath him.

Anna looked at Alex. Alex's eyes widened and then he got a funny look on his face.

"Anna," Alex said, "when Morgan came back into the cabin, it turned to daylight and Charlie disappeared into the kitchen."

"I am warning you," Charlie hollered, trying to sound threatening but sounding terrified instead.

Anna glanced nervously at Charlie and nodded quickly to Alex. "Yah, okay. So what's going on?"

"When Morgan came back into the cabin," Alex continued, "we went back in time to when Charlie first came back here from the fields."

Charlie was near hysterics now. The strange girl and boy knew his name and were talking about his brother, but he had never met them before and he definitely had not heard them walk into his house. *Come back, Morgan,* he thought. *Come back!*

"So we were awake and then we dream-traveled back in time to help a dead boy and his brother and now we have gone back in time while we are back in time?" Anna closed her eyes and shook her head.

"Charlie isn't dead!" yelled Morgan. "He's alive just like

me. And you're in *my* dream and I just want to wake up."

Anna and Alex both turned towards Morgan. Something in their faces made Morgan question himself. "I am dreaming," he said, "right?"

"Please," Charlie begged, tears in his eyes. "Please leave. Morgan is coming back and if he sees you here, he might not let me light the candles tonight."

Anna and Alex went from Morgan to Charlie and then to each other.

"This is madness," said Alex.

But Anna was trying to form a plan.

"It doesn't matter what you think," Morgan said, interrupting Anna's train of thought. "They are coming—whether it's my dream or your dream or no one's dream. I saw them. And they are headed this way."

"What in the world are you talking about?" Anna said, a bit more intensely than she had intended.

Charlie—thinking Anna was talking to him—cowered. "Morgan said I was supposed to protect the cabin and the animals and then he would let me light the candles tonight. I never get to light the candles," he said sheepishly.

Alex slapped his forehead. And Anna calmed him with a hand on his arm.

"No, Charlie. I wasn't talking to you."

Charlie straightened. "But who else would you be talking to?" He looked at Alex who was rolling his eyes in frustration. "I'm not stupid, you know." Charlie scowled.

"Indians," Morgan said simply. "Warrior Indians. They saw me and they are headed this way."

Anna didn't know who to respond to first and so she shoved Alex. "Tell Charlie you're sorry." And then she looked at Morgan. "Are you sure?" she asked.

Alex said a quick apology to Charlie and then turned his attention to Morgan. "Indians?" he said.

"Indians?" Charlie echoed. He moved out of the kitchen towards the front windows. "Where?" There was no one outside that he could see. "You saw Indians?" he asked Alex, worriedly. "Morgan is out there."

"We have to get out of here," Morgan said, urgently. "Even now it may be too late."

Anna had been staring out the window while everyone else was talking, so she was the first to see Pahoma coming down the path that led to the cabin. Her heart stopped. "Indian," she whispered.

At the same moment, Morgan, Alex, and Charlie all looked out the window and saw Pahoma. He was headed down the path—just minutes from the front door.

Charlie screamed. Morgan yelled. Anna and Alex looked at each other.

"What's the plan?" Alex whispered.

"Hide," Anna whispered back. "Quick," she said to Charlie, "where can we hide?"

"Morgan," Charlie was crying. "Where is Morgan? We have to find Morgan."

"Don't worry," Anna said, trying to sound calm. "He is very close. I know it. Where can we hide?"

Morgan was pacing like mad, back and forth in front of the door. "He only saw *me,*" he said to himself. "He doesn't even know about Charlie." He looked up. "Go upstairs to the loft. He doesn't know about anyone besides me. I can—" He stopped, his head dizzy with fear. "I can deal with him. Just go."

Neither Anna nor Alex argued. They simply shuffled Charlie up the stairs with them as quickly as they could.

"Mama Do-Right," Anna whispered under her breath. "What have you gotten us into and where are you?"

Just then, the door opened and Pahoma walked into the cabin. Charlie, Anna, and Alex had made it upstairs just in time and were peeking down from the shadows. Morgan was hiding just behind his parent's bedroom door. He had it slightly cracked open so he could watch to see what the Indian was doing.

Pahoma looked around the modest cabin and frowned. He could have sworn he saw someone inside when he was walking up, but the place looked abandoned. It was a foolish thought to think the other son would have been here after the youngest son had been killed. If the elder boy had survived, he would have fled.

Pahoma sat down heavily on the small couch and breathed long and hard. *I could try and track the boy,* he thought. But he had given his word to the British that he would help track the escaped French soldiers. He had promised two days. But if he waited two more days to track him, the boy's trail would be very difficult to find. *Too difficult*, he thought.

Pahoma hung his head. He was tired—exhausted actually. And he wasn't just tired of this war and all the tracking and fighting. He was tired of his empty world. Since his wife and unborn child had died, nothing held any meaning for him. He had been encouraged by the others in his tribe to find another wife and to start a new family. But no other woman was able to capture his heart as his wife had, and it seemed dishonorable to promise himself to a woman he didn't truly love. And so his lonely heart endured.

"What is he doing?" Alex asked. As far as he could tell, the Indian was just sitting and staring.

"What is he doing?' Charlie echoed, his voice tight with worry. All his thoughts were on Morgan.

Anna didn't reply. She just kept watching him. There was sadness in the Indian. She could feel it. "Why are you here?" she said to herself.

"That is exactly the right question."

Anna turned, startled by the voice she heard. "Mama Do-Right!"

"Mama Do-Right?" repeated, Alex. "Where!"

"Who is Mom Mom Do Right?" whispered Charlie.

Mama Do-Right giggled into Anna's ear. "I am here for

you Anna, as I always am."

"Where are you?' Anna twisted around trying to find evidence of her.

"Where is she?" said Alex, pushing Anna's elbow.

"Who is Mom Mom Do Right?' Charlie repeated.

"Anna, I am not here in physical form. I am a whisper in your ear. But you are on the right course. Just continue. Remember there are no mistakes."

Anna heard Mama Do-Right's giggling in her ear fade until it was silent once more. But Anna didn't have much time to reflect on Mama Do-Right's brief visit, because below them, the Indian had stood and was staring pointedly up at the loft. He had heard Charlie.

Morgan had been watching the Indian's every move from behind the door until he heard whispering in the bedroom behind him. It was when he had turned to figure out what was making the noise that Pahoma had stood and looked up at the loft.

"Who's there?" Morgan whispered into the dark room.

It sounded like someone was calling out his name. A woman. "Mother?" whispered Morgan. "Mother is that you?"

Had his mother made it down from the ridge and into her room without Morgan noticing?

Again he heard his name. It sounded like it was coming

from the wardrobe. Was his mother hiding in the wardrobe? Morgan tiptoed closer to the wardrobe and as he did, he heard his name louder. It *was* his mother.

"Mother!" Morgan exclaimed, trying to contain his joy and relief. He opened the wardrobe and then someone or something behind him pushed him into the small wardrobe.

Mama Do-Right giggled as she closed the door behind Morgan and in a heartbeat Morgan disappeared. A moment later, so did Mama Do-Right.

"Anna, he sees us!" Alex stared down at the Indian, his palms suddenly beginning to sweat.

"No, no, no, no!" whispered Anna. "No, this can't be happening!" And then Anna remembered what Mama Do-Right had told her. "There are no mistakes," Anna said out loud.

"There are no mistakes," repeated Charlie. He was the only one of them who was not afraid of the Indian. Now that he could see the Indian's eyes, there was something very calming and very familiar about him. He looked nice.

Up in the loft, crouched down was the boy—the older boy from the locket. Pahoma reached his hand into his breeches and touched the necklace. Then he looked at Charlie, and motioned for him to come downstairs.

"Come," Pahoma said in his language. "Come."

"Anna?" Alex said, unsure of what to tell Charlie.

"No, Alex. It's okay. There are no mistakes." Anna turned to Charlie. But Charlie didn't wait for her direction. He stood on his own and repeated what the Indian had said. "Come," Charlie said in the Indian's language. "Come." He smiled.

Pahoma's heart softened when he heard Charlie repeat his words. There was an innocence about the boy. Pahoma watched as Charlie made his way down the stairs. He wasn't able to see Anna and Alex trailing behind Charlie, but he noticed immediately that Charlie was very tall. *He's tall like me,* thought Pahoma. And again, he felt his heart stir.

Charlie stood before Pahoma, unafraid and curious while Anna and Alex stood on either side of him. They stood like that for a moment, staring at one and other. There was something in the boy's face which told Pahoma that, although Charlie was a young man in form, he was a child at heart. He looked down. *What am I to do? I killed his mother and now his brother is dead. What will become of this child?*

"What's wrong?" whispered Alex. "The Indian seems upset about something."

Alex's question was answered but not by Anna. Pahoma reached into his breeches and pulled out the locket. He hesitated and then he reached for Charlie's hand and placed the locket in his palm.

"I am sorry," Pahoma said in his own language, his voice thick with grief and remorse.

Charlie looked down at the locket and smiled. "You have Mother's locket!" he said excited. "How did you get her locket? Is she back?"

Anna and Alex exchanged looks. Tears came to Anna's eyes.

"Wow," Alex said, quietly.

Pahoma realized Charlie did not understand. It made his grief that much harder to bear. So he pretended he was pulling back his bow and shooting an arrow. And then he pointed to his back and made like he was falling forward, acting out the moment he had shot Charlie's mother.

"It was an accident," Pahoma said in his own language.

Charlie repeated Pahoma's words, but he still did not understand.

"Charlie," Anna said and placed a hand on his back. "Your mother is... um... your mother is..." Anna looked at Alex.

"Charlie," Alex continued. "Your mother had an accident and she... she died," he said quietly.

Charlie's smile disappeared and he stared at the locket in his hand. He didn't say anything for a long time. He didn't even cry. And then he looked at Pahoma. "She is with the angels," he said. Charlie would cry later over his mother's death. He would cry until his eyes burned and there were no more tears left in his body. But for now, he held it in. At least he had Morgan. "Where is Morgan?" Charlie asked Pahoma. "Have you seen my brother?"

At the mention of Morgan's name, Anna and Alex exchanged looks. They realized that they hadn't seen him since they climbed up to the loft to hide from Pahoma. "Where is Morgan?" mouthed Anna to Alex.

Alex shrugged. "He probably disappeared again," he mouthed back.

Pahoma did not understand what Charlie had asked him. How he wished he had thought to bring his man who spoke the tongue of the British. Pahoma motioned that he did not understand what Charlie was saying.

"He doesn't understand your words, Charlie," Anna explained.

Alex pointed to Charlie's hand. "Show him Morgan's picture from the locket," Alex offered.

"Great idea," Anna said. Mama Do-Right had said there were no mistakes, so maybe there was a connection between Morgan, Charlie, their mother, and this Indian. Maybe the Indian did know something about Morgan. "Do that, Charlie. Show him Morgan's picture."

Charlie handed the locket back to Pahoma.

"No," said Pahoma. "That is yours. Your mother would want you to—" And then Pahoma realized that Charlie was asking about the other boy in the portrait—about his brother. Pahoma hesitated. *What should I tell him? That not only is his mother dead but so is his brother?* The bitter taste returned to his mouth. He swallowed hard. *What will become of this boy now?* Pahoma looked around. Where was the boy's father?

"Where is your father?" Pahoma asked. But of course Charlie could not understand him.

"I don't understand what he is saying," said Charlie, a little frustrated. Pahoma walked around the cabin trying to find evidence that a man lived there. There was nothing in the room that spoke of a man—no pipe, no clothing, no hat, no portrait. Pahoma went into the bedroom.

"What's he doing?" asked Alex.

"What's he doing?" repeated Charlie. Charlie walked away from Anna and Alex and followed Pahoma into the bedroom.

But moments later, both Pahoma and Charlie were back from the bedroom. All Pahoma had found was an empty wardrobe and a small bed. There was no sign of Charlie's father or any man, for that matter. Pahoma's heart was heavy.

"Do you think he knows something?" Alex whispered to Anna. Anna watched Pahoma closely. He walked to the kitchen area now with Charlie at his heels.

"I'm not sure," Anna said, "but he does seem upset about something."

Pahoma returned to the main room and stood near the

small couch. He had found no evidence of Charlie's father during his tour of the house and now he was faced with a big decision. The bitter taste in his mouth was overpowering and he wished he were outside so he could spit.

Charlie, Anna and Alex watched him with curious concern.

And then finally, his mind made up, Pahoma spoke. "Come," he said. "You come with me now." He motioned towards the front door.

"Come," Charlie repeated. "Come with me now." He smiled. He thought they were playing a game.

"He wants to take Charlie to Morgan," Alex said, feeling relieved. Maybe this strange assignment was almost over.

"No, Alex." Anna was staring deeply into Pahoma's eyes. There was something else being said. She was sure of it. *Mama Do-Right, what do I do?*

"Follow your instincts, Anna." Mama Do-Right had returned as a whisper in Anna's ear. "His name is Pahoma. He will take good care of Charlie."

"But... but... where is Morgan?" Anna whispered back. "Charlie won't leave without Morgan."

"What?" Alex said. "Who are you talking to?"

Anna put a hand up to Alex. Mama Do-Right chuckled in her ear.

"Charlie needs Morgan to tell him it's okay to go, but Morgan is gone. Hmm..." Mama Do-Right paused. "I am sure you will figure it out, Anna." Anna felt Mama

Do-Right pat her back and then she was gone.

Pahoma walked to the front door and opened it. "You come with me." He motioned towards the forest that lay beyond the fields. "You will be with me now."

Charlie repeated Pahoma's words—laughing at the strange way Pahoma talked. He was so caught up in the game Pahoma was playing with him that he had all but forgotten about his brother. Until he heard Morgan say his name.

"Charlie, it's me Morgan."

Charlie turned to find Morgan standing behind him, smiling. "Morgan!" he screamed. He threw his arms out, ready to hug Morgan to him, but Morgan stopped him with his hand.

"I can't hug you right now," Morgan said, his voice cracking with emotion. "But I want you to know how proud I am of you. You did exactly what I told you to do."

Charlie looked confused at first and then he smiled proudly. "I watched the cabin and the animals. So that means I get to light the candles!" He clapped his hands.

"Yes, Charlie. But before you light the candles, I need you to do one more thing for me."

Charlie stood up straighter. "Anything, Morgan, because we are a team."

Morgan fought back tears and forced a smile. "I need you to go with Pahoma."

"Pahoma?" Charlie repeated.

At the sound of his name, Pahoma took a shaky step back. He had been watching nervously while Charlie talked to the air. His first thought was that the boy was suffering delusions. But when Charlie said his name, Pahoma became convinced that Charlie was in the middle of a vision. And he knew in that instant that taking Charlie with him and watching over him as though he were his own child was not only the right thing to do, it was the only thing to do.

"The Indian's name is Pahoma," explained Morgan. "He is a good man. He will take care of you."

Charlie shook his head. "But what about you? Where are you going?"

"I have to..." Morgan stopped. What could he tell Charlie? And then he smiled. "I will be right with you in here." Morgan pointed to his heart. "And every night when you go to sleep, I will come and play with you when you dream."

Charlie thought about what Morgan had said for a long moment. And then his head cocked to the side. "So when you come play with me in my dreams we don't have to do any work, we just get to play together?"

Morgan smiled and nodded. "Yes," he said.

Charlie looked back at Pahoma who had tears in his eyes. "Don't worry," Charlie told him. "Morgan is in here." Charlie pointed to his heart. And then he leaned in closer to Pahoma. "And we are going to play every night in my dreams," he whispered. And then he clapped. Pahoma put a reassuring hand on Charlie's back. It was something that Morgan would have done. Charlie smiled.

Morgan felt his energy draining. "It's time now, Charlie. Go with Pahoma. And I will see you in your dreams."

Charlie turned back to his brother and smiled. "I am really brave and I am really strong," he said proudly.

"Yes, you are," Morgan said, a tear rolling down his cheek.

And then Charlie turned back to Pahoma and together they began walking down the path, headed for the forest ahead.

Morgan's body shuddered once, then twice, and then it changed back into its real form. The form of Anna.

Alex had watched the entire transformation from the beginning, when Anna had closed her eyes and looked to be concentrating, to when she transformed herself into Morgan in order to talk to Charlie, to when she successfully transformed back into herself. The only other person he had seen do something similar was...

"Mama Do-Right," he whispered.

Anna, weak from the experience just smiled. "No, Alex. I'm not Mama Do-Right. I'm Anna."

And with that, they both disappeared.

Chapter Twelve

Into The Light

"We're back!" screamed Anna. "We're back!"

Anna hugged Alex so tightly, she feared she might break him into two pieces. But Alex didn't mind. He felt just as overjoyed and relieved as Anna to be back in the comfort of her small bedroom.

"Was that intense or what?" said Anna, finally releasing Alex.

"Intense doesn't even begin to describe it. I mean you changed into another person! It was incredible." Alex grabbed for his notebook.

Anna rubbed her neck. "Yah," said Anna, sighing, "I am just really glad that it's finally over."

"Over?"

Anna and Alex froze in place at the sound of her voice. Together they turned towards Anna's dresser. Leaning casually up against it, absentmindedly inspecting her fingernails, was Mama Do-Right. She looked the same as always: black skin, violet eyes, and white hair on top of her head in a bun decorated with daisies. She wore the same floral print dress as always and, of course, her legs and feet were bare and her toes were wiggling.

"Haven't you forgotten something?" she said pointing her head towards Anna's closet.

As if by magic, Anna's closet door opened. Sitting on the floor inside was Morgan. He was reading Anna's Falling Awake book.

"What are *you* doing here!" Anna demanded.

Morgan, startled, looked up from the book and scowled. "What am *I* doing here? What are *you* doing here? This is my dream, you know. I can be anywhere I want." And then he turned his attention back to the book—ignoring Anna and Alex.

Mama Do-Right chuckled. "He isn't dreaming, Anna," she said. Mama Do-Right smoothed out an invisible wrinkle in her dress. "He died in those fields of a bullet wound to his chest. His mother came to guide him over to the New World, but he was so concerned about Charlie that he—"

"I knew it!" Alex said, interrupting.

"So what are we supposed to do?" Anna said, exasperated.

Mama Do-Right said nothing. She just looked at Anna and smiled. Then she looked past Anna to Alex. "Good job today, Alex." And with that, she winked and disappeared.

Alex walked up to Anna and put a hand on her back. "Sorry, Anna," he said, although he wasn't entirely sure what he was sorry about. He just hated to see Anna so upset.

That's when Anna's expression changed and she smiled. Then she closed her eyes and concentrated. Within seconds, she, Alex, and Morgan were at the edge of the cornfields again. Morgan was more than irritated.

"Why did you have to go and do that?" he yelled. "Now I'm back here."

He was about to throw a fit, when he looked down and saw his own body lying on the ground in front of him in a pool of blood. His body wasn't moving and his eyes were frozen open in a look of shocked surprise.

"What is this?" Morgan said, stumbling back. "What are you doing? Why are you showing me this?"

"You were shot by some French soldiers," Alex said quietly. "You didn't make it."

"You're lying," Morgan cried out. "This is just a dream."

Anna shook her head at Morgan. "He's telling you the truth. But if you don't believe us, ask your mother. She is up there waiting for you." Anna pointed up to the top of the ridge.

High above them, Morgan's mother was waving to her son and motioning for him to come join her.

Morgan looked up at his mother and then he looked back at Anna and Alex. Anna nodded. "Go on," she said. "Ask her yourself."

Morgan hesitated and then decided that maybe they were right. Maybe his mother would have all the answers.

Alex and Anna watched as Morgan made his way slowly up the ridge. His mother did not stop waving at him until she had him in her arms. Morgan fell into her hug and wept so deeply, he feared he would never stop. But then a bright light surrounded them both and suddenly he felt more happiness than he had known his whole life.

As Mary and her son disappeared, she waved one final time to Anna and Alex.

"You're welcome," Anna whispered back.

Anna still had questions. How was it she and Alex had traveled while they were awake? How was she able to change her form like Mama Do-Right? And how many pages were missing from her Falling Awake book? More specifically – *what* pages were missing from her Falling Awake book? But she was much too tired to contemplate all of that now so the answers would have to wait.

Anna reached for Alex's hand. "Come on," she said quietly. "Let's go home."

More with Mama Do-Right,

Anna and Alex!

Turn this page for a first look at the next book in

The Dream Travelers series –

Tail of the Sphinx

Chapter 1

Running Scared

Zahra was running. Through the cold, dark tunnel-like passageways of the Sound Temple – she was running. Her lungs were burning. Her legs were cramping. And her head was dizzy with fear.

Why! Why? Why? Why?! her mind screamed out. But Zahra knew why. She had the luck of the cursed. She was always in the wrong place at the worst time.

Zahra ducked down another random passageway without as much as a glance back. Her feet, shoed in soft hemp sandals, fell as silent as cat paws against the cold stone floor, but her heavy breathing echoed off the perfectly tuned walls (the temple had been designed to amplify sound). Zahra tried to hold her breath, terrified that she had been seen and followed and that her breathing would give her away. But waves of panic pushed hard against lungs that were already on fire from lack of oxygen and within seconds her mouth burst open and she sucked in a long (loud) mouthful of air.

Almost in revolt, her body stopped and refused to take another step forward. Zahra bent over, wheezing for air. Her breath bounced off the tuned walls and echoed back so that is sounded like the entire passageway was gasping for air.

I'm caught for sure, Zahra thought and she fought back another wave of panic so strong it threatened to knock her to the ground. Zahra clasped a shaky hand over her heart and tried to calm herself down.

It's possible I wasn't seen or heard. It's possible that I am not being followed. Zahra paused – giving these reassuring thoughts time to find a home inside her mind. But they were quickly rejected. Even if she hadn't been seen or heard, she *had* seen and heard. And what she had heard and what she had seen was something she could not easily ignore. If – by the luck of the Gods – she was able to make it out of the Sound Temple without being caught or killed, a heavy decision would lay before her.

Zahra closed her eyes and cursed her bad luck. She wasn't supposed to be anywhere near the Sound Temple this evening. In fact, everyone in the valley was down near the river preparing for the upcoming Spring Equinox (the time when the sun was directly above the Earth's equator).

The Equinox was less than five days away and the mammoth offering being built for the Gods was far from being completed. It was ordered that all people (women and children included) were to be on hand to help. And that's where she had been – working along side her mother, her father and her three younger brothers. That is until her mother casually asked how her sound studies were coming. Zahra had nearly dropped her side of the small stone block that she had been carrying with her mother. Her mother's question had been an instant reminder that she had forgotten to collect her stone writing tablets from her class in the Sound Temple earlier that morning. It was an honest mistake. She had put her stone tablets down in a corner so that she could complete a sound exercise and when the exercise was over, she had forgotten to pick them back up. But as honest as the mistake was, neither her mother or father nor her teacher would understand. Zahra was known for her *honest* mistakes and had long since been labeled irresponsible. It was a miracle she had been accepted into the High Priestess training – a fact her parents reminded her of almost everyday. It would be a great dishonor to them if she were expelled. And she was already two warnings into a three warning maximum. One more incident and she would no longer be able to complete the training.

So with the threat of expulsion upon her, Zahra had traded one bad deed for another and had lied to her parents, telling them she was going to the river to fetch them all drinking water. But instead of heading to the river, she had taken off for the Sound Temple. If she ran fast, she had figured, she could get to the temple and back in less than thirty minutes. Sure, she would have some explaining to do (it doesn't take thirty minutes to get water from the river) but she would craft her excuse on her way back.

Zahra straightened up, her breathing quick and shallow. It seemed like a lifetime had passed since she had left her parents. And not only had more than thirty minutes gone by, but she hadn't found her stone tablets either (they weren't in the corner where she had left them which probably meant her teacher had found them before her). This last fact alone would guarantee her expulsion and bring shame and dishonor to her and her family. *If only that were the worst of it,* thought Zahra with dread. What she had stumbled upon just minutes earlier could surely get her murdered.

The thought of her own death brought Zahra to her knees. And that's when she heard the footsteps. Zahra halted her breath and put a sweaty hand on the cold stone floor. The vibration was strong which meant they were close. *The priests!*

Zahra stifled a scream and jerked her head in the direction she had been running before she had stopped. At the very end of the small narrow passage was a wall but before that – to the left - there looked to be a doorway. With nowhere else to run, Zahra stood up to a crouch and – bent in half and wild with fear, she took off down the passageway with her eye on the doorway. Behind her the footsteps got louder. It took everything in her not to scream out loud.

Just when Zahra thought she would burst from terror, she reached the doorway and jumped across the threshold. Once across, she found herself in an empty, darkened cramped room. *A sound chamber!* Her horrible luck persisted with a vengeance. Sound chambers, she had just learned that day, were reserved for meditating with sound. The chambers were built to accommodate three – maybe four people at one time. In all of the temple, the sound chambers were the areas that amplified sound the most. And now Zahra had trapped herself in one of them – a sitting duck for the priests she knew were now after her.

The footsteps were now echoing in the passageway outside. It sounded as if they were running in confident easy strides. *They saw me! They know I'm in here!* Zahra clasped both hands over her mouth to stifle her own breathing. And then suddenly and without obvious reason, the footsteps stopped. Zahra slowly dropped her hands from her mouth. And in that instant a small soft glow of light appeared in the room held up by the hand of a young girl in strange clothing. Standing next to her also dressed quite oddly was a young boy.

"We're here to help you," Anna whispered. But before Alex could nod in agreement, Zahra passed out in a crumple of arms and legs before them.